D1508155

"In every human being, there is no physiologic mechanism as important as thirst. I believe that one of the basic lessons God is presently teaching us is that we have lost touch with our common humanity. We have become disconnected! It is a thirst that is shaking and shaping the world and the church. Mike Mantel, with boldness and Christian courage, invites us in *Thirsting for Living Water* to rediscover through real-life stories our power and combined ability to bring God's healing and redemptive message to a thirsty world. It is a must-read!"

Horace E. Smith, pastor of Apostolic Faith Church in Chicago and attending physician at Lurie Children's Hospital

"This book is staggeringly honest—with a start of Mike's own descent into the 'dark night of the soul.' But it is also refreshingly hopeful—with story after story of God's work in this world and Mike's own journey toward the call on his life. Read of this adventure for yourself and be forewarned that God will soon invite you into one of your own."

Greg Holder, lead pastor of The Crossing and author of *Never Settle*

"We've all had those dark seasons of the soul that author Michael Mantel so vividly describes in his book, *Thirsting for Living Water*. But he provides a refreshing antidote with stories of how God invites us to join his work of redemption—in our homes, our communities, and around the world. I loved his description of how the 'Master Strategist' is always at work with a vision much too grand for us to see. This book is a must-read for anyone who has lost sight of the bigger picture of how we can reach those who thirst for God's living water and do our part to help transform the world."

Lynn Austin, author of *Chasing Shadows*

"This book is a deeply honest story of the pilgrimage—personal and organizational—of one person's call to serve the poor. As a reflective practitioner, Mantel's account rests on his pilgrimage as a Christian called to holistic mission, his continuing efforts to understand the practice and theological basis for both the process and outcomes of Christian social transformation, and his deeply held belief that Christian NGOs can and should 'empty themselves' by choosing to do their work with and through local churches—both those of the poor and the nonpoor."

Bryant L. Myers, senior professor of transformational development at Fuller Theological Seminary and author of *Walking with the Poor*

"I have known Mike for several years, both as CEO of Living Water and as a fellow elder at my church. He is a true follower of Christ. This book not only tells his stories but many other stories from around the world. You will be blessed to read this book and reflect on your stories where Christ has been a faithful father and leader."

Terry Looper, CEO of Texon and author of *Sacred Place* and coauthor of *Work and Worship*

"I have known Mike for many years and have personally observed his lifelong commitment to serve those the world chooses to push aside and/or forget. Mike consistently lives beyond himself, acting to serve the marginalized and oppressed. I invite you to learn more about Mike, who follows the Master Strategist and his love, vision, and redemption through the church."

Santiago "Jimmy" Mellado, president and CEO of Compassion International

"It is with pure joy that I endorse this life-changing book written by my friend Mike Mantel, which will stir up every emotional sensor known to humankind from beginning to end. It takes you on a journey of God's amazing grace through the eyes of living witnesses we can see and speak to in our lifetime! I personally believe this book will lead millions of people from around the world into the life-changing transformation that comes through hearing and accepting the gospel of Jesus Christ, and cause millions more to join our fight in eliminating poverty worldwide!"

Walter August Jr., president of the African American Pastor's Fellowship of Houston, founder of Bethel Family Baptist Church, Houston

"I will never forget my first trip to Africa with Mike. Every part of me changed because of that trip. My heart, mind, body, and soul were opened up to a place and people who now feel like home to me. I witnessed Mike's authentic passion for serving and bringing hope to people all around the world. He has a winsome way of bridging gaps and creating space for healing and hope to rise. Be warned—the words you are about to read will inspire transformation in your life and call you to new levels of courage to change our world. Thank you, Mike, for your message, but more importantly, for living this message."

Jeanne Stevens, World Vision ambassador, lead pastor of Soul City Church, Chicago, and author of *Everyday Brave*

"Have you had a moment in your life when you asked, 'How can a good and all-loving God let something like this happen?' Did it shake your faith? Did it make you wonder if God really exists? If so, this book will take you on one person's journey from faith to unbelief and then to a wider and even deeper faith. Mike not only records this faith journey but then provides steps you can take to ascend or reascend the ladder of faith to God's eternal love and redemption. Let Mike show you how his faith let him bring clean water and the living God to those in need of both around the world."

Jim Moroney, publisher emeritus, *Dallas Morning News*

"*Thirsting for Living Water* moves us through faith and work with realism. The journey of the dark night of the soul is intensely personal, and Mike Mantel has shown how to embrace it in the midst of leading a superb organization."

Samuel E. Chiang, cofounder of the Global Centre for Giftedness and catalyst for orality with the Lausanne Movement

"*Adventure* is the operative word for Mike Mantel's new book. Honest, raw, and inspiring. The gripping stories herein capture the profound adventure that all of us are in for when we finally release control of our lives and ask Jesus Christ a truly terrifying question: 'What are you doing . . . and how can I be a part of it?' Mantel's candid stories of doubt, difficulty, and transformation will invite and inspire you to ask that terrifying and adventure-filled question for yourself. Do not be afraid. Read it."

Matthew Kaemingk, Mouw Chair of Faith and Public Life at Fuller Seminary, and coauthor of *Work and Worship*

"I felt as though this book was written for me. I devoured it in one sitting. You will be encouraged and strengthened as I have been by seeing how the deep tapestry of God's plan is woven by the great Master Strategist into the amazing and glorious masterpiece of his grace in our lives. Thank you, Mike, for writing this book for me, for people like me, and for many others whose lives and experiences will resonate with your journey."

Goodwill Shana, president of the Association of Evangelicals in Africa, founder and senior pastor of World of Life International Ministries

"This book is an inspiring story about what's right with the church today, and Mike Mantel is the perfect person to tell it. Mike's journey will excite you, delight you, and most importantly invite you to join with other fun, smart, dynamic, compassionate people who do God's work through the church here, there, and to the ends of the earth."

James Ludema, dean of the School of Business at Calvin University and author of *The Appreciative Inquiry Summit*

"*Thirsting for Living Water* is a must-read. It reminds us of the bigger puzzle that each of us is part of. The deeper we follow God's lead, the more the unexpected happens for the greater good of humanity. Ba Mike brings out the divine plans in an ordinary way for every reader to marvel at God's doing. Pass it on; it's a great read and reminder for our time."

Princess Kasune Zulu, member of Parliament, Zambia, and author of *Warrior Princess*

"With a missionary essence and biblical grounding, Dr. Mike Mantel shares compelling stories of transforming experiences that bring hope and redemption. *Thirsting for Living Water* invites in-depth reflection on your own journey and calling as an agent of change in the Kingdom."

Tony Miranda, pastor and president of the Hispanic Baptist Convention of Texas

"I have not read a book since *Love Does* that will inspire every reader to get up out of their chair and go live out the adventure of truly following Jesus. I laughed, cried, celebrated, repented, and grieved a broken world as I followed this beautiful journey. Don't just read this; buy a copy for your family and friends."

Chris Seay, lead pastor of Ecclesia Houston and author of *A Place at the Table*

"A warm invitation to look at our lives through the grace and direction of God. Mike uses his story, including the hardest seasons of his life, as a model to show us how to pay attention to what God could be up to. With reflection questions to frame each chapter, this book could be used as a great guide for discussions for everyone from youth groups through adult education and leadership teams."

Mary S. Hulst, university pastor at Calvin University

"This is a significant book for uncertain times in which our comfort zones have been shaken and we wonder, What is next? It's an honest book about personal suffering, doubt, and faith. The reader will connect and identify with Mike's experience and will grow in faith, finding encouragement and hope in following our Lord Jesus Christ."

Ruben "Tito" Paredes, director and professor of anthropology and missions at the Orlando E. Costas Graduate School of Mission in Lima, Peru, and former general secretary of the Latin American Theological Fraternity

MICHAEL J.
MANTEL

FOREWORD BY
RICHARD STEARNS

THIRSTING
FOR
LIVING
WATER

FINDING ADVENTURE
and PURPOSE *in* GOD'S
REDEMPTION STORY

An imprint of InterVarsity Press
Downers Grove, Illinois

InterVarsity Press
P.O. Box 1400, Downers Grove, IL 60515-1426
ivpress.com
email@ivpress.com

InterVarsity Press® is the book-publishing division of InterVarsity Christian Fellowship/USA®, a movement of students and faculty active on campus at hundreds of universities, colleges, and schools of nursing in the United States of America, and a member movement of the International Fellowship of Evangelical Students. For information about local and regional activities, visit intervarsity.org.

All Scripture quotations, unless otherwise indicated, are taken from The Holy Bible, New International Version®, NIV®. Copyright © 1973, 1978, 1984, 2011 by Biblica, Inc.™ Used by permission of Zondervan. All rights reserved worldwide. www.zondervan.com. The "NIV" and "New International Version" are trademarks registered in the United States Patent and Trademark Office by Biblica, Inc.™

While any stories in this book are true, some names and identifying information may have been changed to protect the privacy of individuals.

The publisher cannot verify the accuracy or functionality of website URLs used in this book beyond the date of publication.

Cover design and image composite: David Fassett
Interior design: Jeanna Wiggins
Image: outdoor water spicket: © Mint Images / Getty Images

ISBN 978-1-5140-0292-6 (print)
ISBN 978-1-5140-0293-3 (digital)

Printed in the United States of America ♻

InterVarsity Press is committed to ecological stewardship and to the conservation of natural resources in all our operations. This book was printed using sustainably sourced paper.

Library of Congress Cataloging-in-Publication Data
Names: Mantel, Michael J., 1960- author.
Title: Thirsting for living water : finding adventure and purpose in God's
   redemption story / Michael J. Mantel ; foreword by Richard Stearns.
Description: Downers Grove, IL : InterVarsity Press, [2021] | Includes
   bibliographical references.
Identifiers: LCCN 2021024255 (print) | LCCN 2021024256 (ebook) | ISBN
   9781514002926 (print) | ISBN 9781514002933 (digital)
Subjects: LCSH: Missions. | Church history--21st century.
Classification: LCC BV2063 .M343 2021 (print) | LCC BV2063 (ebook) | DDC
   266--dc23
LC record available at https://lccn.loc.gov/2021024255
LC ebook record available at https://lccn.loc.gov/2021024256

P   19   18   17   16   15   14   13   12   11   10   9   8   7   6   5   4   3   2   1
Y   37   36   35   34   33   32   31   30   29   28   27   26   25   24   23   22   21

To the

storytellers

of God's

faithfulness

CONTENTS

PART THREE: TO THE ENDS OF THE EARTH

FOREWORD

Richard Stearns

I MET MIKE IN 1998 when I joined World Vision as its president, and I enjoyed serving with him over the next decade. He had been leading our fundraising teams in the Midwest for several years when we began to innovate new, relational engagement platforms for churches in Chicago and then across the United States. In *Thirsting for Living Water*, you will read about some of the great adventures that grew from his call to serve the church by equipping it to fill the hole in our gospel through action with the poor in our major cities and around the world.

On my first visit to Chicago, when Mike picked me up at O'Hare Airport, I was immediately impressed (perhaps not positively) by his 1987 Grand Marquis, and my impression was deepened when it sputtered to a stop next to the valet at the downtown Sheraton where we intended to launch Vision Chicago with hundreds of ministry partners, city officials, and donors. While I still can't shake that first impression, I experienced that night and for years to come the creative and polished effectiveness of a diverse team of outstanding colleagues and volunteers made possible through Mike's visionary and relational leadership.

I wish Mike would have written this book years ago. It has given me more insight into what (or who) was driving him to press forward into new and sometimes unorthodox approaches to ministry; why he pressed so hard to apply World Vision's international relief and development approaches in cities in the United States; why he spent so much energy building relationships in both urban and suburban churches; why he continuously invited business and ministry leaders to serve together on advisory boards or to build new organizations; how he and his colleagues were drawn into the passion to stop HIV/AIDS and to bless people with water.

Mike has a unique vantage point both to observe and to invite people to join God's redemption story through their churches. I witnessed this in Chicago as he and his teams invited larger suburban churches to build relationships and serve alongside networks of smaller urban churches. I witnessed it in cities throughout the United States where churches linked arms with each other to be a blessing across the street and around the world. Mike continued and expanded this powerful work of joining and equipping churches when he joined Living Water International as their president and CEO in 2008.

When Mike and I talked about his vision for this book, I encouraged Mike to use his personal and organizational stories to serve as the engine to pull along the big story of how God continues to invite us to join him as he redeems and reconciles his world. Mike has accomplished this masterfully in *Thirsting for Living Water*. And even better, he invites us, his readers, to reflect on and share our own stories as we build a chorus of what is right with and possible with and through Christ's church.

I have been blessed to lead in both businesses and ministry. I have experienced and seen firsthand that God prepares us and invites us to participate in his work in whatever state we find ourselves. *Thirsting for Living Water* brings to life how our faithful and loving God accomplishes his amazing purposes through his body, the church.

I encourage you to join Mike as he takes us on his descent into the dark night of his soul, then back in time and around the world to validate that God truly is *the* Master Strategist. He is always with his

people and always working to redeem the world through our relationships with him and with each other. In *The Hole in Our Gospel*, I
challenged readers to consider what loaves and fish we can bring to
Jesus with our own time, talents, and treasure. I think Mike's page-
turning journey in *Thirsting for Living Water* will stir your own memories and hopes—and could very well be the tool God is using to
prepare you for the great adventure that he has prepared for you in
his redemption story.

INTRODUCTION

A S PRESIDENT AND CEO OF Living Water International, I work with churches across America and around the world that have enabled over six million people to access safe water and experience the living water of Jesus Christ since 1990. Here in the United States, I work with some church communities where people say church is where they come alive and change the world. The whole family participates, and they invite their friends to join them. In some of these communities, nonreligious people get involved—because they want to change the world too.

I also see other kinds of churches. I see churches where people *want* to live into their highest ideals of "church," but they're bored, they feel stuck, or they feel like God is distant and uninvolved in their lives. In my experience, the first kind of church has identified where God is at work in the world and has found its role in that work, while the second kind has not.

My vantage point at Living Water International gives me a unique perspective on this dynamic. Part of our work is to help churches identify how God is moving in people's lives, communities, and the world and to equip them to connect with that work. We do this with churches in the United States and across Africa, South Asia, Latin America, and the Caribbean.

I have a lot of sympathy for people who are not excited about church. There was a time when I felt that way, too. In the prologue, you will learn how in 1987 in Senegal, West Africa, I got my first glimpse of how God is poignantly involved in human affairs.

I did not go to Senegal to find God. I already knew God was an all-knowing and all-powerful Creator who sustains all things. I went to Senegal to help someone install a windmill pump on a water well because it seemed like an exciting adventure. Once there, seeing people dance with joy because they now had safe drinking water, I experienced the work of God as a master strategist who makes impossible things happen and who invites us to participate. I was undone to witness that God not only loves the Senegalese, but he included me in his redeeming work. I said yes to the God of this vision, and the next thirty years became one adventure after another on assignment for the Master Strategist who has guided me every step of the way.

Exactly thirty years later, in 2017, everything I knew about God as the Master Strategist began to unravel with such force it sent me spinning into the silence and darkness of doubt. In six short months, I faced death, economic crisis, leadership doubt, and natural disaster. After decades of Christian ministry leadership, my foundations were shaken: Maybe God is *not* the Master Strategist, inviting us to join him as he redeems the world, and providing for us as we go. Maybe God isn't involved in our affairs at all. Perhaps I had built my life on an illusion, and I had been inviting others to do the same all along. It seemed as though all the evidence was stacked against me. I saw no evidence of a coming resurrection, and big leadership decisions hung in the balance. This type of spiritual crisis is often referred to as the "dark night of the soul," a phrase taken from a sixteenth-century poem by Saint John of the Cross.[1]

I had to dig deep for answers. *Thirsting for Living Water* is about the new hope I found in the light on the other side.

||||||||||||||||||||||||

This book contains many of my stories; I hope that you are able to find your own stories while reading it. Most importantly, this is the story of the work that the body of Christ is doing in the world today.

Part one—"You Will Be My Witnesses"—consists of four reflections drawn from my descent into the dark night of the soul that catalyzed the rest of this story. The anecdotes in this section will introduce you to my journey and invite you to reflect on your own journey, as well as your orientation toward the Bible, love, faith, hope, and the witness of God you are bound to become. "

Part two—"In Jerusalem, and in All Judea and Samaria"—is a soul-searching journey back in time. These reflections are about some of the forces that shaped my faith and perspective of the church through the concentric circles and outward expansion of family, community, city, and the world.

Part three—"To the Ends of the Earth"—is my journey around the world. It tells stories of God doing extraordinary things through ordinary people like you and me, and ordinary churches like yours and mine: "there," "here," and across the unified, global body of Christ. I believe the vision that emerges will fill you with new hope for the church that is more alive and filled with potential today than ever before in history and that invites you to participate in its richness.

As you engage with each of the twelve reflections, I invite you to activate personal recollections my story prompts in you. As you consider the questions at the end of each reflection, capture key elements of your own story to later share with someone you trust.

Join me on this journey and emerge with a clearer vision of what is right with the church today. My deepest hope is that these stories—mine and yours—will be a catalyst to experience a deep, flowing river of hopeful reflections of how God is actively transforming this world through you, his people, the church, as we work together to bless others at home, among our near neighbors, and even to the ends of the earth.

All proceeds from this book will help Living Water International empower churches to mobilize communities to help them to gain access to safe drinking water, sanitation infrastructure, and improved hygiene and to experience the good news of Jesus Christ.

A GLIMPSE OF THE MASTER STRATEGIST

L ET'S BEGIN WITH the story of how I ended up in Senegal getting a glimpse of God, the Master Strategist who delights in our collaboration in his work to redeem all of creation.

It all started with a job I got working for a pizza tycoon because my most pressing goal at that stage in life was to get rich.

I was young, and I wanted to learn everything I could about business, so I found a job working for the only billionaire in Ann Arbor, Michigan. His name was Tom Monaghan.

Tom's father had passed away on Christmas Eve when he was just four years old, and he came under the care of the Catholic sisters at the St. Joseph Home for Children. Like many boys of his era, Tom dreamed of becoming a Major League Baseball player.

Fifteen years later, Tom's dreams had changed. He now dreamed of becoming an architect, and he ran a little pizza business to pay tuition for architecture school at the University of Michigan. When he started losing more money on the pizza business than he was losing on his education, Tom dropped out of architecture school to give his business the attention it needed. In so doing, Tom figured out that people wanted pizzas delivered to their homes, parties, and dorms. He invented a stackable, insulated box that allowed delivery people to stack pizzas, keep them hot, and deliver more pizzas on every run. Targeting college campuses with the promise of quick delivery, his company grew into the second-biggest pizza business in the world. At one point, he was opening three new Domino's Pizza stores a day.

Tom never got to be a baseball player, but he bought the Detroit Tigers baseball team. He never got that architecture degree, but he built Domino's Farms, a nearly one-million-square-foot office park inspired by the design principles of the famous architect Frank Lloyd Wright—and that is where I come in.

I was director of operations at Domino's Farms, which not only housed the pizza company's headquarters but also included a working farm that hosted fifty thousand children a year to teach them how pizza dough comes from wheat, sauce from tomatoes, and cheese from cows. We had a petting farm with a herd of American bison, pygmy goats, and a museum of steam-powered farm equipment. We had the world's biggest collection of Frank Lloyd Wright artifacts and a classic car museum. Tom was always finding ways big and small to live out his architecture dreams.

One Thanksgiving, Tom had us set a half-mile-long Thanksgiving dinner table and cover it with Butterball turkeys as far as the eye could see. One Christmas, he set aside a million bucks to create the world's longest nativity scene. As director of operations, that became my job.

We created a two-mile-long nativity scene. It was an extraordinary undertaking, culminating in a six-week Christmas light show. Nearly a quarter-million people came out to see it, and they dropped $117,000 of pocket change into the charity buckets we put out for our local, national, and global charity partners.

We invited representatives of nine charity partners to Tom's $2 million office with leather floors, mahogany walls, and silk ceilings, and gave each of them a $15,000 check. One of those checks was earmarked for a windmill water pump in Africa. Two weeks later, I got a call from a man named Max.

"Mike," Max said, "I'm going to Senegal to put up a windmill—want to come?"

"Yes!" I said, purely out of a sense of adventure. Everything I knew about Africa had come from *National Geographic* magazine, missionary speakers at my church, and the movie *Casablanca.*

Max told me that in Senegal the desert was eating up a mile of good farmland every year, and that he had a vision to take it back.

"We're going to be like the Dutch," he said. "We're going to put a line of windmills across the Sahel Desert, and we're going to take that desert for Jesus!"

I loved the whole idea. My father is Dutch, and the windmills Max intended to replace were from Argentina, like my father-in-law. Max was pushing my buttons, and he did not even know it. I also thought he was crazy, which made me want to go to Africa with him even more.

Boarding for departure, the *Air Afrique* logo on the plane caught my eye, and I felt like the coolest "man of the world" since Humphrey Bogart's character Rick Blaine in *Casablanca.*

When we landed in Senegal, I got into an old blue Mercedes taxi and was driven for hours through the desert. People I saw were tall and thin, with fine features. Their complexions were dark and beautiful, and they wore long robes. To my inexperienced eyes, it seemed like a *Casablanca* desert scene—I was not in Ann Arbor anymore.

Our taxi took us to meet with community leaders. I became friends with the local marabout, a Muslim holy man. I gave him a flashlight as a gift, and he gave me a ring that I still cherish to this day. The local chief was a young Senegalese man with big glasses. A missionary kid with long hair showed me how to skim off the top of the bubbling yogurt they drank. A couple British roughnecks drilled a water well, and a former army colonel from Vietnam, Lộc Lê Châu, showed me around.

We went into people's homes and I was moved by their generosity. Everyone shared whatever they had with no concern for themselves. I watched my marabout friend eat a handful of peanuts, and a couple fell to the ground. I would have let them go, but he picked them up and dusted them off to eat. Every morsel of food was so precious, yet people were delighted to give it away.

Figure 0.1. Celebration at the opening of a windmill-powered well in Senegal, 1987

We had been there about a week when Max and I finished assembling the windmill. When he removed the safety pin that kept it from spinning, a gust of wind came along, the windmill turned, water flowed, and the entire community of Wolof people burst into song and dance. I had never seen anything like it. Women made ecstatic sounds of joy, men danced, and even crusty old Max burst out singing, "Hallelujah, hallelujah!"

A choir of little Wolof kids joined in, imitating Max as they all danced along, shouting, "Hallelujah!" and "Praise Jesus!"

Lộc Lê Châu stood up on a rock and preached about Jesus and the water of life. He told the gospel story in French, which was translated into Wolof for the crowd and English for me.

By now I had seen how access to safe drinking water results in better health, more freedom for women and girls, more food, work, time, education, money—better lives in every way. It was clear to me what all the dancing, singing, and praising Jesus was about. I sat on a sand mound in the shade of a scrubby little acacia tree, thinking about the utterly impossible things I had witnessed.

Lord, I prayed, *you are amazing! You are a master strategist who makes impossible things happen!*

I thought about how none of this would have happened without all the people who had been involved: Tom Monaghan and the Christmas light show, the people who dropped coins in the buckets, crusty old Max, Lộc Lê Châu, the marabout, the village chief, the British roughnecks, and the missionary kid who showed me how to scoop the bubbly yogurt. These players were not fully aware of the bigger picture to which they contributed, but what came into view for me was nothing less than lives being transformed. I thought about what an impossible feat it was that these Wolof people now accessed safe, clean drinking water from hundreds of meters beneath the desert floor, and how many of these people had heard the good news of Jesus Christ for the very first time. I had a personal spiritual moment in which a series of thoughts flooded my head and heart:

I am not alone.

God knows me.

God loves me.

There is no need for fear.

God is at work restoring our world.

God invites me to take part in that work.

We are a community.

I can participate in God's work and invite others to do the same.

I reflected on the way I was part of this story. My choosing the charities for the Christmas light show had played a pivotal role linking Tom and Max to this community. God was the Master Strategist of *my* life too. I wanted to be more a part of God's work.

God, I prayed, *I want to work for you, because you are the Master Strategist. I don't want to work for a billionaire or a great human—no human can orchestrate things so completely or miraculously as you, God.*

That feeling—the experience of impossible, beautiful things coming together through our discernment of the will of God, the Master Strategist—became something I wanted to experience over and over. I thought of my young daughters' joyful cries from the playground, when they would beg me to swing them again and again. I was like a child at play with God, shouting, "Swing me again! Swing me again!"

In answer to my prayer, God led me on a journey over the next thirty years that flowed through one adventure after another, in US inner cities, in suburbs, overseas in Africa, South Asia, Latin America, or the Caribbean—until my dark night of the soul, when I stopped hearing from God and felt utterly alone.

"Swing me again!" I shouted . . .

. . . and my father died, my wife, Natalie, was diagnosed with cancer, financial crisis threatened the Christian ministry entrusted to my leadership, and a natural disaster devastated our city.

"Swing me . . . ?"

PART ONE

YOU WILL
BE MY
WITNESSES

MY FATHER LEFT AN ADVANCE DIRECTIVE

Come, you who are blessed by my Father; take your inheritance,
the kingdom prepared for you since the creation of the world.
For I was hungry and you gave me something to eat,
I was thirsty and you gave me something to drink,
I was a stranger and you invited me in,
I needed clothes and you clothed me,
I was sick and you looked after me,
I was in prison and you came to visit me.

MATTHEW 25:34-36

M Y DESCENT INTO the dark night of the soul began with the death of my father.

My father's death was not untimely. He was ninety-three years old and had lived a good life. My mother had gone before him, and he was in pain. He was ready to be with God, if for no other reason than to be free of the catheter he was forced to use late in life. Nonetheless, the death of one's father always inspires a kind of pensive woe, conjuring memories and mixed emotions.

My father and I did not always get along when I was young. He was always at work, and he was hard for a child to know. I felt him to be distant, uninvolved in my life. I thought he was harsh, demanding, and did not care about things children care about.

Although all of that could be said of my relationship with my human father, all of it could also be said of my relationship with my heavenly Father. Before this story is all over, I would love both of those fathers, leave both of them, and invite both of them back into my life.

This story is about honoring my father's advance directive in the midst of so much confusion as he approached his death. It is about honoring what he wanted of me, even when it was not easy. As you have probably already guessed, this reflection is also about honoring the "advance directive" our heavenly Father left us, even when it isn't easy.

As you read this story, I invite you to recall a challenging or confusing time in your life when God's word in Scripture offered you comfort or clarity.

ıιιιιιιιιιιιιιιιιιιιιι

It hurt to see my father's mouth so dry. His teeth were just dry bones now. Never again would they grace us with a smile. His lips were turning black.

My dad's world had been closing in on him for years now. He had once defied Nazis by offering refuge to Jewish neighbors during World War II. He once crossed a vast ocean alone to get from war-torn Holland to the land of opportunity. Now he was confined to a shrinking body that lost moisture with every breath. For the rest of his life now he would shrink in weight, hydration, and vigor until he died under the hum of the fluorescent hospital lights.

My wife, Natalie, and I were at lunch with my mentor and Living Water's cofounder Gary Loveless and his wife, Stephanie, when we got the call. My father was on his way to the hospital. By itself, this was not a cause for immediate concern. Dad loved a good ambulance trip to the hospital. The lights, the wild ride on a reclining bed in a climate-controlled truck, being chauffeured, carried, wheeled around to meet people with fresh new faces—this is the most exhilarating thrill available to a ninety-three-year-old man in his condition.

Only this time he was in that ambulance because he had suffered the stroke that would take his life. We later learned that he had been transferred en route to a special stroke unit ambulance to begin treatment sooner for this life-threatening event. When we got to the hospital, they called us into the emergency room for questions.

My dad had insisted that Natalie draft a set of legal documents that included an advance directive to provide clear instructions to implement during the very confusing and emotional time when death is pending. He had an advance directive, but there were gray areas. His wishes were clear, but there were circumstances he could not have foreseen. The doctor explained the situation and said it was our decision—did we want to intervene or let him struggle on his own to the end?

We needed to act fast if we wanted to intubate and feed him through an IV. The clock was ticking. I felt the burden of Dad's brain cells dying with every passing moment as I called my out-of-town brothers. An eternity passed from one phone ring to the next. I was relieved once we were all on the line. We decided it would best honor Dad's personal wishes, and his written request, to let nature take its course. We decided to let him die.

The doctors didn't say it like that. Had they been Dutchmen like my father they would have spoken plainly, saying what they meant with no prelude or fancy terms, but that is not how physicians talk. They spoke in what seemed to me to be code. Everything spoken in a hospital becomes an exercise in discernment. Words for conditions and procedures are foreign, euphemisms abound, time is scarce, and there is no Rosetta Stone to help you sort things out. You just do your best in the midst of all the gray uncertainty.

Judging by what the doctors had said, I thought my dad would die within the hour. I did not know if he could hear me, but I told him I loved him. He held onto my arm, which I took as a sign that he was still there. I told him everything I wanted to say. Then we sat in silence. Minutes went by, then hours. Nurses performed their routines. Fluorescent lights buzzed. Other patients shuffled about. I wanted to know what was going to happen, but the emergency room is a busy, high-pressure place, and when the staff members have time to answer questions, it isn't always clear what they are saying. You sort things out as you go.

After some time, Dad was moved to a regular room and we decided to go home and get some sleep. We came back the next day, and our time together was the same as the day before. Realizing that this may take time, we resolved to visit him every day. We sang old hymns to him. We talked to him. We read psalms to him. I began to feel guilty for letting him die this way; doubt crowded in.

Day after day his mouth dried out. Every time he exhaled, a little moisture was released into the sterile hospital air. Days had passed since his last drink of water. It seemed to me that dehydration would play a role in taking his life, which was ironic. In my role with Living Water International, my vocation is to quench both physical and

Figure 1.1. Holding my father's hand as he slowly passed away

spiritual thirst, but I felt useless for that here. I felt a pressure slowly building with each passing day. Time gave rise to uncertainty. I no longer knew if I was making the right calls or the wrong ones. I had no idea what was going on inside my father's head or his heart. I also had no idea what he needed spiritually, and we had promised not to intervene by meeting his physical needs. That promise was more difficult to keep with each day that passed as Dad's lips blackened over his dry tombstone teeth.

I had no way to know what he could think or feel. I did not know if he was hungry as we gave him nothing to eat, or thirsty as we gave him nothing to drink. I did not know if he felt alone when we left, or sick, or estranged, or imprisoned in his slowly dehydrating body. To the extent that he could feel anything at all, I saw that my father suffered the same afflictions Christ endured on the cross—hunger, thirst, loneliness, illness, estrangement, and imprisonment.

In those days, I thought a lot about Jesus' teaching about the sheep and the goats. Long ago, Natalie and I had made that passage from Matthew's Gospel a central aspect of our lives, so I had thought about the twenty-fifth chapter of Matthew a lot throughout my life. Now those words took on new dimensions.

In his Gospel, Matthew presents twenty chapters of Jesus' teaching and healing building up to a series of discourses that start to feel more serious, more apocalyptic, and more consequential than the ones that came before. Then, the last of those public teachings before Judas betrays Jesus is the one of the sheep and the goats. It is a story about how we treat the thirsty, hungry, naked, sick, lonely, and imprisoned. Those afflictions assumed new poignancy now that I knew my father would suffer them all until his coming death.

In the vivid image of a shepherd sorting sheep from goats, Jesus describes God sorting out the nations at the end of time. Those who fed the hungry, gave water to the thirsty, invited in the stranger, clothed the naked, cared for the sick, and visited the prisoner, he says, will inherit the kingdom prepared for them since the creation of the world. The others will "go away to eternal punishment" (Matthew 25:46).

It's harsh. I don't claim to know exactly what Jesus means, but his language is strong. As his people, Jesus expects us to feed the hungry, give water to the thirsty, invite the stranger, clothe the naked, care for the sick, and visit the prisoner. When we serve him by serving the people who suffer, we will be invited to enter the kingdom prepared for us since the creation of the world.

Jesus said that when we do those things for the least of our brothers and sisters, we do the same for him. As Natalie and I began to take that teaching to heart, we began to see that for those living on less than two dollars per day, safe drinking water was their most fundamental need. We began to see how safe drinking water empowers people to address other needs—how it is the first step in a staircase that leads to the capacity to reach their God-given potential. More and more people's access to safe, clean drinking water became our focus as we saw firsthand how access to it not only quenched thirst but also enabled people to grow food, kept them from getting sick, and provided a vital public space where churches could invite strangers into communion. So we dedicated our lives to helping offer a drink to the thirsty—except for the thirsty man in front of us.

Jesus' teaching that "whatever you did for one of the least of these brothers and sisters of mine, you did for me" is beautiful (Matthew 25:40), but I doubt the disciples appreciated it as they watched their Savior die. Jesus suffered in all those ways on the cross: he was hungry and thirsty—a stranger to this world, rejected by people who had stripped him naked, inflicted suffering beyond any illness, and imprisoned him on a Roman cross. When Jesus said, "I am thirsty," the disciples probably did not think about quenching their Lord's thirst by offering a drink to the least of their brothers and sisters (John 19:28). I bet they just looked up, saw a dying man, and had no idea what to do.

I had no idea what to do for my dying father. I was glad I had invited my dad to live with us at the end of his life. I was glad I got to know him as an adult. It was not until later in my life that he embodied compassionate fatherhood for me. In those later years, he became my teacher and my confidant when life was difficult. He was a good counselor who could strip away distraction and get right to the heart of a matter. He had given me life. Now I just watched as day after day his lips darkened, his breathing became more difficult, and I felt more out of sorts, wondering whether I had done the right thing.

Then he passed away.

"I am thirsty," the apostle John records Christ's words from the cross (John 19:28). "It is finished," and with that Jesus bowed his head and gave up his spirit (John 19:30). That was how it was with my father too. He was thirsty, then it was finished—for me, it was a relief.

Those days in the hospital had been a bewildering blur of emotion, jargon, confusion, farewell, and decisions I felt unequipped to make. With the clarity of hindsight, I now see that I can look back on those days without regret because *I knew exactly what my father wanted.* Not only that, I realized long afterward what a privilege it was to be by his side in his pain, to be the one entrusted to carry out his advance directive in real time.

In this case, I knew what my father wanted because he had created an advance directive. In the midst of fear, doubt, confusion—all along—I really knew what he wanted; I just needed to implement it. I was grateful that he had provided clear, written direction because in the moment it was hard to see what he would have wanted. If I hadn't had that, every intervention I approved would have led us further from his goal, which was to be free of his body and return to God in peace without unnecessary delay.

We are in the same situation with God. We hear God's voice sometimes, but other times we don't. Often, the times we don't are times when our circumstances, our emotions, our pride, and so many other things create a subterfuge that makes it difficult to see our way. But he has not left us without an advance directive. He has left us a written record of what our heavenly Father wants us to do. When our judgment is clouded, the Bible will provide clarity.

The Bible is a treasure trove of advance directives from our heavenly Father. God calls each of us into his master plan through his written word. When we are confused or looking for guidance, God speaks to us through Scripture. While each of our calls might be different, the bottom line is that we find out what God wants us to do and then do it.

For Natalie and me, Jesus' words in Matthew 25 had always provided clarity about what God wants us to do: to offer food to the hungry, water to the thirsty, hospitality to the stranger, clothes for the naked, care for the sick, company for the imprisoned—and when we offer those things, we do the same for Jesus himself. As long as there are suffering people on earth, at least some portion of the Christian life must be oriented toward those concerns.

I don't understand this as a burden, but as an opportunity to take my place in the kingdom prepared for me by my Father. As difficult as it was to honor my dad's advance directive, I had been privileged to be the one who sat with him in his last days and hours. He had chosen me to be that person. And God has chosen each of us to carry out his advance directive. Every time I see a person or a community identify where God is at work in the world addressing the needs of his people and joining him in that work, I see them gain vitality, adventure, and meaning.

Now that my father was gone, it was finally time to get back to our own long-neglected lives, including our mission to see Jesus thirsty in the least of our brothers and sisters and to offer them a drink. Before that, though, Natalie needed to go in for that mammogram appointment she had missed while we cared for my father.

Reflect

Mike's father's advance directive offered him clarity and comfort in a difficult time. Our heavenly Father's "advance directive" does the same through Scripture. Mike cites Matthew 25:34-36 as God's "advance directive" asking us to offer food, water, hospitality, clothes, care, and company to those in need. What "advance directive" has God left you in Scripture?

Write

Call to mind a challenging or confusing time when God's "advance directive" through Scripture offered you clarity or peace. Write that story, recording how you felt in that time of need, how the words of Scripture helped, and how you felt afterward.

Share

Share your story with someone you trust and ask them to do the same. Make note of the various ways God reveals what he wants of us through Scripture.

LOVE IS A
SPIRITUAL PRACTICE

God is love. Whoever lives in love lives in God, and God in them. . . .
There is no fear in love. But perfect love drives out fear.

1 JOHN 4:16, 18

D ESPITE ALL THE medical advancements we have made in the last century, the death rate among humans remains at 100 percent. The Bible begins with a story about Adam and Eve letting death into the Garden of Eden, and we've been managing our anxiety about that circumstance ever since. Consciously or not, to be human is to live with a certain amount of pathos about death. Predictably, my father's death prompted reflections on my own mortality. I thought my attitude toward death was pretty healthy, or at least it was in February 2017. By March, my every thought was haunted by the specter of death—not mine, but that of my wife, Natalie.

Natalie's cancer diagnosis was the next nudge in the direction of my dark night of the soul. Some of you, no doubt, have experienced the horror of cancer. If you haven't yet, it is tragically likely that you one day will. According to the National Cancer Institute, 38.4 percent of Americans will be diagnosed with cancer in their lifetime.[1] I pray that the tragedy of cancer never hits close to home for you, but if it does, may God grace you with all the love, prayer, and care we experienced.

"Perfect love drives out fear," writes John in his first epistle. I do not imagine there are many fears greater than that of losing the one you love. As that fear gnawed at me day by day, it was at times accompanied by a more perfect awareness of love. There were even moments when that love drove out all our fear. With those moments came an awareness that the love we experienced had always been available to us and was worthy of more deliberate practice. "Whoever lives in love," after all, "lives in God."

"God is love." Those three words may seem too easily dismissible— they sound like a trite platitude worthy of an embroidered pillow. But they express something about the nature of reality, the ground on which our faith is built and upon which Christ builds his church.

As you read this story, I invite you to bring to mind a person or persons with whom you have experienced love. Whether it was the love of a partner, family member, friend, or the divine love of God, how did you know that it was love and how did you practice it?

IIIIIIIIIIIIIIIIIIIIIIIII

Thirty-three years go by in a snap.

The warm April dawn poured gold across Natalie's skin as she slept. I could still see the girl I married thirty-three years ago. She was also every woman I had loved since—my partner, friend, confidante, collaborator, the one at whose side I think, plan, and dream. I had been in love with Natalie the student, adventurer, mother, teacher, lawyer, and best friend to our daughters. She was the relational force who held us all together. Marriage had given me all those Natalies, as well as the one who slept beside me under the warm spring sun. These mornings watching her sleep were the sweetest I had ever known. Every second of this precious time together warmed my heart. These morning moments were the eye of a storm that whirled around us now, their serenity defiled only by my fear that she could be dead in a month. Everything had become so painfully sweet since the cancer diagnosis.

We had always assumed that I would die first. I fly a lot. I am always traveling to distant corners of the world, being exposed to strange diseases. I work in impoverished countries and in the wake of tsunamis, hurricanes, earthquakes, political strife, violent crime, and religious conflict. Or, we thought, there was always the danger in things I eat or drink.

Every once in a while, I will end up in a rural African community, celebrating a new water infrastructure we built together. It's a special event, a celebration of having saved lives as precious to others as Natalie's is to me. On such occasions, we are often celebrating years of building bridges across ethnic, religious, and financial barriers that separate us from a vision of global unity we call "the body of Christ."

Imagine the scene: Community elders seat me at a rough wood table lashed together with leather strips. They welcome me by draping a robe over my shoulders, and people laugh in delight to see a big *mzungu* (person of European descent) dressed like a village elder. All eyes are on me, then the chief hands me a gourd of raw, fermented goat's milk.

It's nutrient-rich, and people have been drinking it for millennia, but the thought of it turns my uninitiated stomach. Our church and community mobilizer, who is deeply aware of local tradition, says the insult of refusing this gesture would embarrass the respected chief, and people would talk about it, which would negatively affect the reputation of our local church partners. In case you are wondering what one does in such a situation, you do the same thing Jesus did when facing distress—you pray that the cup may pass. I drink a polite amount, and I get sick; or more often, I am fine. A seemingly "death-defying" situation like this becomes a colorful little tale to tell later, but it is not cancer.

My father had passed away in February. Within a few weeks, death loomed over us again. Natalie's diagnosis was in March. Our lives had become a blur in recent years as getting my dad where he needed to be, having dinners with him, and taking him to church were added to the tasks of raising our children and facing challenges at work. Then suddenly we were visiting him in the hospital every day, interpreting medical jargon, singing psalms to a mute old man, and having doubts about all our decisions. Then there were memorial services to arrange, communication with family and friends to manage, all while navigating a serious financial crisis at work. As always, Natalie held our family together with her signature strength. In so doing she had postponed a mammogram that was already years overdue.

Neither of us had thought much of it. Natalie was the healthy one. She was disciplined, determined, strong-willed, focused, and always made the right choices. She is physically even stronger than she looks, and she has an extremely high tolerance for pain. There is nothing fragile about her. The sum of these qualities made her seem invincible, at least to me.

Figure 2.1. Natalie and I embark on another adventure

Natalie is beautiful but not vain. She exercises nearly every day. She does not exercise to look good but because she takes the long view of things, and she plans on going the distance. It seemed like such a miscarriage of justice that someone who worked so hard would be invaded by mutant cells that multiplied and grew each day and would continue to do so until they killed their host.

When Natalie went in for that overdue mammogram, the technician saw abnormal tissue. They said she needed a biopsy. When the doctor called and asked her to come into the office to discuss the results, she knew where this was going.

When Natalie told me she had cancer, I lost any sense I once had of a solid foundation to stand on. Time suddenly meant nothing. I had no idea how much time we had left. I would have no way of knowing for many months to come. My mind raced with every scenario, outcome, and question: Had I loved her well enough? Did I show her how much I care? Had I done enough for her? Did work ever get between us? Would she continue to be the relational force that drew our family together? How would we care for our daughters? Or, how would I? How would our daughter Katie take this? Maggie? Abbi? Libby? Was I saying and doing the right things, even in this moment? What would we do with the time we had left?

I knew nothing about treatment. I had no idea if she could die in a day, a week, a month, six months. I had no way to get a grip on time.

As a leader, my job is to translate vision into action that is anchored in time. At Living Water International we did that through a prayerful process of spiritual discernment and strategic planning. We take about a year at a time to engage people around the world in a bottom-up process of prayer, listening, and engaging local resources and expertise. We discover our strengths together, then dream collectively to envision a shared future we are excited about. Then we turn that dream into a plan for every aspect of our work, divided into quarterly goals for the next five years:

Goal, goal, goal, year.
Goal, goal, goal, year.
GOAL . . .

Then we do it again. Life develops a certain rhythm this way. But now I had no grasp on rhythm or time itself. Instead, I was back in the bewildering, lifeless fluorescent milieu where experts speak in code. We got little bits of information, one or two at a time:

Abnormal cells.

A tumor.

Biopsy.

Cancer.

Breast cancer.

Lymph nodes.

If the cancer gets into a lymph node, you have to pull it out.

Lymph nodes spread the cancer, and if it gets into one it will get into others.

There is a clear to milky-white fluid called *lymph* flowing through our bodies. It carries white blood cells called *lymphocytes*. They fight infection and kill abnormal cells. All this time Natalie and I owed our lives to a milky fluid I had not even known existed. Now we lived in fear that the wrong cells could get into that milky fluid and leave our daughters without a mom.

We needed a doctor. Natalie's primary care physician had given us a name, but it was unknown, and we were desperately searching for *something* known. So Natalie called a friend who is a physician and asked for her recommendation—the same name. We called to make an appointment but were disheartened that it would be six weeks before she could be seen. Could we stand six weeks of knowing that cancer was eating away at her body? Should we look for another unknown doctor? We prayed for guidance. When the phone rang, we were stunned to hear "the doctor has just had a cancellation next week, so she could fit you in then."

All this time I was grasping at an understanding of time, but there was no grasp to be had. There were only probabilities. Sixty-five percent of women this age, with this cancer, at this stage, with this intervention are alive five years later. But were we in the sixty-five percent? Or the thirty-five percent? There's no way to know. If we were on the wrong side of the equation, I would lose her whatever the odds. The numbers became meaningless as my fear increased, further eroding my foundation.

I am an optimist by nature. If I have a professional superpower, it is the ability to help people develop a positive view of the future. Now I found it nearly impossible to feel positive about the future. My mind chattered constantly, conjuring little hells of regret with numbers, odds, thoughts of a tragic end, ceaseless doubt, and fear that the worst could happen.

But there were moments, like that golden April dawn as I watched Natalie sleep, when love drove out all my fears. In those moments we were in the eye of the storm that whirled around us, the place where "perfect love drives out fear" (1 John 4:18).

In a cruel and twisted way, cancer had led me to truth. As a divine gift, Natalie had always been this precious. Love had always been this precious. Life had always been this sweet, even when I had failed to feel it. God loved me through Natalie, and he loves each of us more than we could ever love the other. This mind—the one flooded with love as I watched Natalie sleep—this was my right mind. This was the love that I would practice.

How then would we live?

How then would we *practice* the preciousness of love?

I took a few days off work to relandscape the backyard with Natalie. It occurs to me now that gardening for those days was a deeply spiritual practice. The love we felt so poignantly under the shadow of death had always been available to us. Too often, work or other circumstances had kept us from experiencing that love deeply and intentionally. What could be more worthy of deliberate practice than love?

If, as we read in Scripture, "God is love," then to intentionally practice love is to participate in who God is. "Whoever lives in love," John continues, "lives in God, and God in them" (1 John 4:16). Nothing could be more fundamental to the Christian life than the spiritual discipline of celebrating and spending time together in love with each other and with God.

Natalie put on her gloves. The soil was full of life, and all the spring flowers were in bloom. There were begonias, bluebonnets, and morning glories. We put raised beds for tomatoes in the backyard. Pressing roots into the soil side by side, every moment was precious. Such moments had always been accessible to us, but it took a cancer to make me aware of it.

Everywhere, there was such love all around. I felt it personally, Natalie and I felt it as a couple, and we felt it as a family with our daughters. Friends and people at church showered us with love expressed through home-cooked meals, cards of encouragement, and help around the house. There was nothing we could not have asked of them. We were always in their thoughts and prayers. It was a time when those words, "thoughts and prayers," often just hollow sounds people make in times of tragedy, were deeply meaningful for us. We really were in the thoughts and prayers of our friends, families, coworkers, and church. For us, because of our work, our church extended across the globe. People in all those regions were praying for us and we could feel it. This depth of care is what we want for everyone.

Breathing in and breathing out on that April dawn, she was the same girl I had married thirty-three years before. Our relationship was more precious than it had ever been, our family more cherished, memories more wonderful, life sweeter, our friends more overflowing with love—and all this love was God moving in and through his people.

God's love is constant. It is all around us, even when we do not feel it. Love is not just an emotion we feel but a reality we practice with each other and through the church. God's greatest commandment through his advance directive of the Scriptures is to love God with all your heart, soul, mind, and strength and to love your neighbor as yourself (Matthew 22:35-40; Mark 12:28-34; Luke 10:27). The apostle Paul prioritized love as the greatest asset in the church over tongues, prophecy, knowledge, and faith (1 Corinthians 13:1-11).

The full light of day now glared as I watched Natalie sleep. I do not know how long I had been watching her, reflecting on the preciousness of love, when she turned in her sleep, exposing a dark, radiated patch of skin.

Reflect

"God is love. Whoever lives in love lives in God, and God in them."
(1 John 4:16)

Take time to reflect deeply on that passage from Scripture—does it have any implications you had not previously expected?

Write

"There is no fear in love. But perfect love drives out fear."
(1 John 4:18)

Write down one thing you will do to prioritize and practice love this week with God and with others.

Share

Think of someone in your life through whom you have experienced love. Tell them how that experience of love has driven out fear or helped you experience God.

YOUR FAITH WILL BE TESTED

Some of the wise will stumble, so that they may be refined,
purified and made spotless until the time of the end,
for it will still come at the appointed time.

DANIEL 11:35

HOWEVER STRONG YOUR FAITH, life will sooner or later provide circumstances that cause you to feel distant from God and alone.

"My God, my God," Jesus exclaimed from the cross, "why have you forsaken me?" (Matthew 27:46). If even Christ faced such moments in his life, we can hardly expect to sidestep them in ours.

After the loss of my father and Natalie's cancer diagnosis, the next slide into my dark night of the soul was caused by the seemingly insurmountable challenges at Living Water after a long period of exceptional growth. After thirty years of active spiritual discernment in leadership, I began to feel alone. I found it destabilizing to doubt my own judgment and role. My stories are not the worst stories, and they certainly are not the only stories of turbulent, devastating circumstances, but they distressed me.

As you read this story, I invite you to recall a time in your life when you felt alone or felt God was distant, silent, or absent.

||||||||||||||||||||||||||

When I received the invitation to serve as Living Water International's president and CEO, I was elated to invest my remaining time and focus all my energy on the two most important things in life: water and "living water," the gospel of Jesus Christ.

Ever since that spiritual experience by the water well in Senegal—the vision of God as the Master Strategist inviting me to participate in his redemptive work—I believed that God had been inviting me to focus on these two issues.

In Living Water International, I discovered a community that shared this twin focus, as described in its mission statement:

> Living Water International exists to demonstrate the love of God
> by helping communities acquire desperately needed clean water,
> and experience "living water"—the gospel of Jesus Christ—which
> alone satisfies the deepest thirst.[1]

For the most materially poor people in the world, no single intervention is more essential to physical health than helping communities gain access to safe, sustainable drinking water. All subsequent forms of development depend on access to water. Consider the impact safe, plentiful water has on health, education, economy, and the lives of women and girls.

Health. Half the hospital beds in developing countries are occupied by people suffering from diseases such as diarrhea, guinea worm, trachoma, and schistosomiasis caused by poor water, sanitation, and hygiene.[2] Diarrhea is a leading cause of malnutrition and the second leading cause of death in children under five years old. Each year diarrhea kills 525,000 children.[3]

Education. Each year children miss 443 million days of school due to water-related illness. Of those, 272 million are lost due to diarrhea alone.[4] Lack of safe drinking water is responsible for the loss of 1.2 million years of childhood potential each year.

Economy. On average, every $1 invested in water and sanitation yields $4 in economic returns in the form of reduced health care costs and increased productivity.[5] Plentiful water enables people, especially women and children, to grow food and to spend their time working or going to school.

Women. In Africa and Asia women walk an average distance of 6 kilometers, or 3.7 miles, every day to collect water.[6] Women and girls around the world spend 200 million hours *every day* just collecting water, often in unsafe environments. That is a cumulative 22,800 years, every day, just hauling water.[7]

Imagine the human potential that would be unleashed on earth if everyone just had access to safe drinking water! Now imagine water being offered in Jesus' name as a sign of God's kingdom. Surely you are beginning to see a vision of life "on earth as it is in heaven" (Matthew 6:10)!

Just as I came to understand access to safe drinking water to be the single most important contribution to *physical* health and wellbeing, I came to understand the experience of living water—the gospel of Jesus Christ—as the single most important contribution to *spiritual* health and wellbeing, including my own.

In 2008, when Living Water's board and its visionary cofounder Gary Evans invited me to engage that ministry's global staff in discerning God's will for the future, I was offered a unique opportunity to integrate and apply my PhD studies and all my professional experience to date.

Alongside new friends among the partners and staff from the United States, Africa, South Asia, Latin America, and the Caribbean, we embarked on a year-long process of discernment using a process called Appreciative Inquiry[8] to discover, dream, design, and deliver a strategic plan we called *Watershed: Cultivating Our Strengths for Growth & Impact.*

We organized a series of prayerful listening and envisioning summits with people representing every aspect of Living Water's work—implementing partners, donors, board members, foundations, and staff, including well drillers, hygiene instructors, church workers, and grassroots organizers from around the world—contributing to our collectively discerned vision for our future.

At each of these summits, everyone listened to the story of someone from a completely different background. Millionaires listened to community organizers. Ugandan church workers swapped stories with American megachurch pastors. Well drillers shared ideas with mission trip coordinators. Everyone shared the story of his or her experience of Living Water International at its best. Many of the stories were as life changing as my "water of life" experience in Senegal. Everyone's strengths were drawn out, and everyone had a role to play in the new reality we were becoming. Through a variety of storytelling exercises in various configurations—and through theater, art, prayer, song, shared meals, and strategic planning—God revealed to our global team a divinely inspired and collaboratively constructed vision of the future that we turned into a plan for action.

The future envisioned by Living Water's global team was bold. New science had been coming out at the time from the World Health Organization, UNICEF, and governments around the world. People were now saying that improved hygiene behaviors and sanitation infrastructure could save even more lives than just first-time access to the safe water on which they depend. Living Water had always been a good water-well drilling organization, but the global team collectively discerned that God wanted us to venture into the more challenging areas of sanitation infrastructure, hygiene education, behavior change, and even more effective strategies for monitoring, evaluation, and sustainability. Most exciting of all, the team wanted to drastically increase their commitment to empowering churches to more effectively demonstrate and proclaim the good news of Jesus Christ.

This bold new vision required us to rethink our fundraising model. Water well sponsorships were relatively easy to fund at $5,000 or $10,000 per project. Our new plan, however, would require us to invest

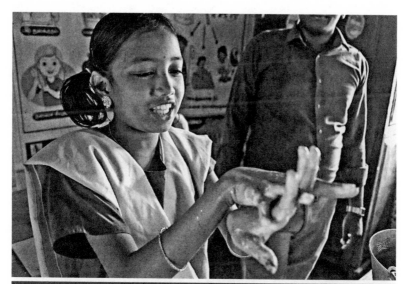

Figure 3.1. Improved hygiene behaviors save even more lives than water access alone

not just in projects but in *people*—their ongoing training, education, discipleship, mentorship, and empowerment.

We calculated that to accomplish our new and ambitious goals, we would need to double our revenue over the next five years. That is an ambitious growth plan for any nonprofit at any time, but we were also in the middle of a recession! The International Monetary Fund said it was the biggest economic downturn since the Great Depression, but not even *that* tempered the dreams of our team. We had prayed, listened, and experienced the leading of the Holy Spirit together. As a leader, I was particularly dependent on this faith. There is no way I could have trusted the bold decisions our team was making without it. The philosophical shift the *Watershed* process led us through was too profound to endure without deep faith that everything was in the hands of God, the Master Strategist.

"Water, for life, in Jesus' name" became our new tagline as God expanded our horizons in four primary ways.

The first thing was to globalize. We had been a small US organization funding a variety of partners around the world, but we had a vision to become a global organization with skilled leadership and informed decision-making in the field, where the work is happening. Over the next years, with the capable leadership of Board Chair David Welch, we expanded our board representation from across the United States and from countries in which we operate. We made 250 hires across a range of ages, including national leaders who understood local languages, customs, and the spiritual landscape of their unique environments in ways our founders never could. We put every Living Water operation in the hands of skilled local teams—church and community mobilizers, health promoters, water technicians, and support staff. We updated and harmonized our agreements, standards, processes, tools, and technology; and we digitized reporting, using smartphones to monitor our work from anywhere, at any time.

Next, we more intentionally integrated water and the Word. We adjusted our budget to invest more in gospel proclamation, more in church mobilization, and more in discipleship. Doing so, we mobilized thousands of people in churches around the world to integrate the life-saving power of water, sanitation, and hygiene—a demonstration of God's love—with verbally sharing the gospel of Jesus Christ—the proclamation of God's love. Church leaders were motivated to act—not by a paycheck but by the divine invitation to love their neighbors.

Third, we expanded our focus from water to WASH. WASH is the acronym for Water, Sanitation, and Hygiene. We continued to provide water access by helping communities drill water wells, harvest rainwater, or build larger-scale water systems with pumps, tanks, towers, and distribution through pipes and taps. Sanitation keeps water safe from its source to the moment it's consumed. Good sanitation changes how and where people collect and store water, wash and dry dishes, keep animals, and most importantly, how they dispose of waste. Hygiene refers to the personal practices that keep us healthy—things like handwashing with safe water and soap at critical times: after changing diapers or using the bathroom, and before preparing or eating food.

Finally, with the help of visionary partners like The Rees-Jones Foundation, we started focusing our work in geographically defined areas, where our teams stayed "in the neighborhood" for five years to serve in ways that multiplied impact. We called these WASH Program Areas (WPAs).

Concentrating our work like this cultivated long-term relationships, developed trust, built capacity, and enabled sharing the gospel in more meaningful ways. Through WPAs we gained the ability to monitor and evaluate improvements to water access and behavior change over time, and then to incorporate our learnings into future strategies for sustainability.

Working in WPAs enabled us to coordinate with established and emerging partners and collaborators from churches, schools, clinics, government agencies, and other nonprofits at local,

Figure. 3.2. Coordinating elements of WASH Program Areas (WPAs)

county, and national levels. Together, we built and implemented an empowering environment where grassroots church mobilization efforts have the support they need to succeed.

WASH Program Areas gave us more opportunities to equip churches with skills they could apply to other big needs in their community and to teach others to do the same—all of us learning and growing over time.

Each challenge we faced honed our skills, built resilience, and sharpened servant leaders to address the next issue.

We implemented new operational, administrative, and fundraising processes all at once. We launched new pilot programs, developed global standards for every aspect of our work, and updated policies to manage and reduce risk. We improved financial and project reporting, transformed our fundraising model, and opened regional offices across the United States.

You can imagine how proud I was of our global staff as they executed all this change during a severe recession. Even as we watched nonprofit sector peers go out of business, our financial health remained better than ever. We could not understand how some of our nation's biggest financial institutions collapsed while Living Water doubled its revenue. We became the organization we dreamed of becoming—and it was exhausting.

I had not anticipated how difficult it would be. Every challenge unveiled a dozen more. People were getting tired, and I was no exception. Sustaining this pace while caring for my father, then through Natalie's cancer diagnosis, began to take a toll on me personally.

We had outrun the global financial crisis since 2008. Even as Fannie Mae, Freddie Mac, Lehman, and Citigroup tanked; the American auto industry flopped; and housing-related assets plunged in the wake of the subprime mortgage crisis, we had stayed strong. But in 2017, it caught up with us.

In great part we had stayed strong because the price of oil had remained high throughout the financial chaos. Founded in Houston, Texas in 1990, Living Water International had been filling its board of directors with generous, committed visionaries talented in business, finance, administration, strategic planning, and every skill needed to run a global operation like ours for a quarter century. When you look for those kinds of minds in the energy capital of the world, you are bound to end up working with some people in the oil industry and their charitable foundations, churches, and social networks.

When I joined Living Water in 2008, oil peaked at $145 a barrel; it dropped to $110 in 2012 and then crashed to $26 in 2016. Take a moment to let that sink in: $145 to $26 per barrel! Friends and supporters went out of business. Those who remained in business no longer had disposable income. Thoughts about charitable giving were replaced by thoughts of survival. Business owners worried about the fates of their employees and their families. The oil crash had an enormous impact on our board, our donors, and our bottom line, but the financial storm was even worse than that.

Interest rates were now at an all-time low. People who still had money started putting it in longer-term real estate deals where it would be tied up for years. People who had money in foundations were not giving it away because their investments were no longer growing. By law they have to give away 5 percent of the value of their net investment assets each year to keep their legal status. Now that 5 percent payout rule was cutting into their endowments. As everyone watched their charitable foundations shrink, their excitement about giving their money away also shrank.

Feelings of insecurity were compounded by a contentious 2016 election year. Everyone on both sides feared the election of the other candidate who, they believed, was only looking out for himself or herself. Imagining the worst-case scenario if their candidate lost, people drew inward and held on to what they had in order to weather the storm they believed was coming.

When a ministry like ours has cash coming in each year, it can pay for learning, create an environment of possibility and accomplish effective ministry. Leaders can afford mistakes, encourage innovation, create an environment of personal growth, and nurture visions of opportunity. Everything feels achievable.

Cash is the life blood of an operation, but it is also the fruit of our decisions and our labors. If cash is down, thirsty people continue to suffer. They do not gain access to safe water nor do they experience living water. When cash remains low, regardless of the cause, the senior staff person is responsible. Even when revenue is flat, expenses continue to rise to meet the needs of the thirsty. To discontinue paying business expenses such as cost-of-living increases, equipment replacement, system improvements, and investments in multi-year programs makes it more difficult to attract and retain the highest caliber staff, pursue excellence, and encourage appropriate risk taking. It is amazing how far our teams can lean forward into significant challenges and opportunities to transform the lives of the thirsty when confidence is high—and how difficult the daily grind becomes as it diminishes. Anyone who leads an organization feels the enormous responsibility of meeting the daily commitments we have to our constituents.

Since 2010 we had been growing at 15 percent a year compounded. With that growth in mind, we had made commitments and promises to not only the thirsty, but our church and community partners, donors, and staff and their families—current and future. But now we were spinning our wheels just to stay flat while our costs continued to rise. Our staff looked for cost-of-living salary increases, and I wanted them to have it. But even a modest salary increase seemed impossible when we were already behind budget with no idea how we could possibly make it up. We had already tried everything. The environment felt like one of less opportunity, less flexibility, less security, less vision, and less hope.

Many of us began to act out our stress behaviors: pointing fingers, questioning intentions, diminishing others, emphasizing others' weaknesses to appear strong. Exhaustion and financial insecurity breed suspicion and scrutiny. People start to second-guess one another's decisions, interpret things negatively, and grumble. Camps of like-minded people start to form, and people only speak to others who agree with them. Disputes arise. Rival camps begin to undermine each other. Grumbling starts to spill over to the board, planting seeds of doubts. None of this was unique to Living Water International. I had seen the same across organizations in my personal experience and in my formal study of organizational behavior, and I hoped to avoid what I'd observed in other places.

I would like to say I hovered over all this like Jesus napping in a boat on the Sea of Galilee, but that was not quite the case. Normally I am a warm, engaging visionary, and I tend to encourage and empower others. In a meeting, I'll get a sense of the room and make decisions based on my gut. Under stress, though, I constrict, take control, and do more things myself. Rather than trust my gut, I send staff scrambling for more data. Often this results in digging up evidence that the future will be grim, which compounds discouragement.

One negative flare-up especially got under my skin. It was related to our efforts to demonstrate and proclaim the gospel. During all those years of growth it really felt like God was on our side. But now, a few people started wondering why it seemed like God was not on our side anymore. Someone suggested that perhaps God was no longer blessing us financially because we were not being faithful. Could God be punishing us for shying away from sharing the gospel?

This simply was not true. Over the preceding years we had increased our annual investment in gospel proclamation strategies 500 percent. We were empowering churches around the world to demonstrate and proclaim the gospel in more authentic, relational, faithful, Christlike ways than ever. We were seeing churches help heal rifts between Tutsis and Hutus in Rwanda. We were seeing Christians and Hindus embrace the good news of Jesus together. We were helping churches proclaim the good news of Jesus by serving the hungry, the thirsty, the stranger, the lonely, the sick, and the imprisoned. This all came about as a result of the faithful, prayerful discernment of our global staff, some of the most faithful Christians I have ever encountered. Yet even our faithfulness to God's Great Commission was in question?

The loss and fear in my personal life was draining my reserves, and the compounding challenges in my ministry life began to erode my confidence in the critical question of my leadership. This was all especially destabilizing because it felt like things were spinning out of control in precisely the areas of my strengths. My unique strength had always been my ability to see and collectively build a viable future; to engage corporate systems to help people find a positive focus; to harness core strengths; and to align people and systems to move toward a collective vision. Now I felt isolated and underequipped. In this climate of scarcity, fear, and doubt I started to question the memory of my spiritual experience in Senegal all those years before. I started looking for data. The evidence seemed to suggest that maybe I had misread things, and worse, a perilous doubt began to creep into my mind—maybe God was *not* the Master Strategist who would provide for our work. If I had misread that, what else had I misread? Maybe I *am* alone. Maybe God does *not* know me and love me in such a personal way. Maybe God is *not* intimately involved in the affairs of humankind, redeeming our world, and inviting us to join that redemptive work.

Turning to Scripture for direction, I read from Daniel. "Some of the wise will stumble," Scripture assured me, "so that they may be refined, purified and made spotless" (Daniel 11:35). I did not feel wise in that moment, nor did I feel like God was refining me, or purifying me, or making me spotless. I knew the truth of these words, but I doubted that my faith was deep enough to weather the storms I faced. Our workplace was under terrible stress even though we had faithfully sought God's will and offered ourselves to his work. My father's death was still fresh. Natalie had cancer. I was haunted by the possibility of her death, and so were our daughters. Financial peril loomed. I began to question my own leadership. I could not bear to fail the colleagues and donors who chose to link arms with us. I thought of all the people whose lives we would fail to touch with safe drinking water and with living water, the gospel of Jesus Christ. I thought of infants dehydrated by diarrhea, sick children, empty school desks, and mothers burdened by the fading eyes of their babies. I thought of all the men and women around the world whose families were counting on us.

Reflecting on this time, I had few answers and less hope. I knew that God had me in his hand, but I could not feel it. I knew that everyone has a dark night, but this was different. This was *my* dark night. My view of success and failure was limited to a universe that revolved around me—failure loomed large through the lens of doubt. This was a time that God's view of my success and failure would have been invaluable, but I could not see it. Only as I pen these words can I see in hindsight that God was, in fact, present and working out his plan, preparing me for dawn.

I needed a sign from God, an olive branch to assure me there was another shore out there. I cried out in prayer, asking God for a sign that he was still faithful.

God's response . . . was Hurricane Harvey. Or rather, that was what happened next. Harvey devastated our city, workplaces, economy, and homes.

Reflect

Remember a time when you felt abandoned or alone and remember the thoughts, emotions, and sensations associated with that experience.

Write

Jot down any glimpse you caught of how God was present and at work through that circumstance in some way you could not see at the time.

Share

Share your recollections with someone you trust. Discuss ways that God might have been at work in your life, in someone else's life, or putting you in a holding pattern until some other events occurred.

WAIT FOR THE GIFT PROMISED BY THE FATHER

But you will receive power when the Holy Spirit comes on you;
and you will be my witnesses in Jerusalem,
and in all Judea and Samaria,
and to the ends of the earth.

ACTS 1:8

WHEN IT RAINS, IT POURS," THEY SAY.

As I navigated all the storms that surrounded me—death, cancer, financial crisis, relational stress, professional turmoil, spiritual doubt, and all the others unmentioned herein—it was a literal storm that finally cast me into my dark night of the soul. This was not just any old storm. It was one of the costliest storms in US history, Hurricane Harvey.

As you read this story, I invite you to recall your own dark night of the soul and identify to whom you looked for the comfort, insight, and power to carry on.

||||||||||||||||||||||||||

Natalie and I were in Chicago when Hurricane Harvey made landfall. Our flights back to Texas were among the thousands canceled by the storm. We stayed in close touch with family and friends by phone and watched weather reports on television. We saw news of devastation across South Texas—roofs ripped off homes, winds gusting up to 132 miles per hour, and a six-foot storm surge as the Category 4 hurricane crept east toward Houston. The storm, spanning nearly three hundred miles, dipped back into the Gulf of Mexico, gathered water, then dumped it again on America's fourth-largest city.[1]

Every family in Houston was like Noah's, preparing an ark for the storm. In the Energy Capital of the World, people dusted off generators, getting ready to lose power. Water and nonperishable food vanished from grocery store shelves. Plywood disappeared from hardware stores. People shuttered windows and gathered food, water, medicines, flashlights, batteries, and important documents; they filled cars with gas, then waited to see what would happen next.

Water poured down at up to six inches per hour. The rainfall was literally off the charts. The National Weather Service added two new colors to its weather maps, doubling the upper end of its scale to capture just half the storm's maximum rainfall.[2] It was the wettest tropical cyclone in United States history.[3] Meteorologists said Harvey dumped so much water it began to suck that same water back up and dump it on the city again.[4]

Floodwaters left 336,000 residents without electricity, damaged 185,000 homes, and forced more than 30,000 evacuees to run, swim, or row for their lives.[5] Casualty reports began to pour in; every day the death toll rose. The storm poured 19 trillion gallons of water over Houston and Southeast Texas. The amount of water that flows over Niagara Falls in two weeks fell on Harris County in just four days.[6] Climate writers called it "a 1,000-year flood event unprecedented in scale."[7] Newscasters spoke of its "Old Testament wrath," calling it "a disaster of biblical proportions."[8]

When the airports reopened, Natalie and I flew home to our devastated city. One of Living Water's cofounders and board members,

Becky Morris, had lost her home. Our IT director had lost his. Everyone at Living Water had friends or family who were suffering. I suggested that everyone take time to help family and friends, then get involved in the rescue and response efforts of their favorite church.

I called my friend Chris Seay, pastor of Ecclesia Houston. Ecclesia is a creative, visionary church, so I knew they would already have something in motion. Few people in the world love their city as much as Chris loves Houston. Chris is also a big thinker who makes big things happen. I knew he could use someone like me to keep him company and bounce around ideas with. I called him up and said, "Chris, let me be your wingman and wheelman for a week."

The first task was to rescue people from flooded homes. The Coast Guard and FEMA got to work, and not far behind them the Cajun Navy rolled into town in high-clearance pickup trucks towing shallow-draft craft. Perhaps recalling Houston's hospitality during Hurricane Katrina, ad-hoc volunteer groups from Louisiana and East Texas began to deploy civilian rescue missions. Volunteer dispatchers monitored the Cajun Navy Facebook page, relaying rescue requests to boat pilots via Zello, an app created by an Austin startup that enables smartphones to be used as walkie-talkies.[9] Responding to the overwhelming need, churches started their own citizen rescue teams. According to FEMA, the combined efforts of local, state, and federal first responders resulted in the rescue of 122,331 people and 5,234 pets.[10] After lives were secured, our attention turned to material damage.

The next urgent task was to muck out flooded homes. Nearly every home in a flood zone had to be stripped to the studs in a race against time before harmful molds took over. Teams cut up fallen trees, removed debris, dragged everything out of homes, cleared walls, ripped out cabinets, stripped floors, and tore down drywall. The flood respected no status. Rich and poor, Black and White, luxury homes and low-income homes near the water were all flooded.

Prior to the hurricane, a couple of aging churches had signed over their buildings to Ecclesia to be revitalized for a new generation. Ecclesia turned one of those buildings into a disaster response staging area. It became a warehouse for distributing hurricane response equipment. Film crews got to work shooting videos to inform people, describe needs, and enlist volunteers. Chefs from Paper Co., a café that dedicated its profits to Houston's homeless, volunteered to keep people fed. Mattress Mack, the owner of a local furniture store, donated bedding so the church could offer dorm-style accommodations for all incoming volunteers. People affectionately called the operation "Hotel Jesus." Each week it housed hundreds of volunteers anxious to participate in Houston's rebirth from the floodwaters.

Eighteen churches from across Texas, fifteen from the Midwest, thirteen from the West Coast, and twelve from the East Coast sent volunteers and supplies to Ecclesia. Every day for months these churches armed battalions of house muckers to be dispatched throughout the city according to needs communicated through church networks. This hub of church activity alone helped muck out more than six hundred homes across the city.

One day as I drove Chris around, he got a call from the Christian relief and development organization World Vision. They had an enormous gifts-in-kind program, and they had just made a big deal with Costco to distribute donated construction materials, new home furniture and appliances, and tools for mucking houses. All they needed was a downtown distribution center.

A while back, Ecclesia had purchased an old two-story building that had once been a strip club and bar. Ecclesia saw its potential to offer new life in downtown Houston, but plans came to a halt when the Texas Department of Transportation, TxDOT, said they would need to demolish the building for freeway expansion. Chris envisioned this property as an ideal distribution center. I used to work at World Vision, so I was familiar with how they structured their contracts and what they would need. In fact, I had overseen a similar warehouse in Chicago called The Storehouse, a collaboration among World Vision, corporate donors, and African American and Latino church leaders who served families in need through home improvement projects. With Natalie's legal assistance and my experience, Chris negotiated a deal that worked for TxDOT, World Vision, Costco, Ecclesia, and the City of Houston to provide supplies for the beleaguered people of Houston.

A church member who owned a construction company secured the building, set up lights, fixed the roof, and covered broken windows with plywood. In no time at all we had a 50,000 square-foot, rent-free, downtown warehouse from which World Vision and its partners would distribute $9 million in supplies to 311,000 flood victims in underserved parts of the city. The whole process was one of seamless and efficient cooperation among church leaders, government agencies, corporations, nonprofits, and flood victims. In this time of crisis, the sixty or so churches that made Hotel Jesus happen were a model of the body of Christ healing our city in the way God intends for us to heal the world—and this was just one among hundreds of such church efforts across the city.

The church is an often-overlooked player in disasters like these. Throughout the city, churches opened their doors as shelters, signed up volunteers to care for neighbors in need, and turned open parking lots and church warehouses into distribution sites for relief, clean-up, and reconstruction efforts.

The White House Office of Faith-Based and Neighborhood Partnerships published a toolkit called Partnerships for the Common Good.[11] In it they wrote, "nonprofit organizations, including faith-based and community organizations, play a vital role in both preparing for a disaster, and in ensuring an inclusive and participatory community-wide recovery from a disaster." Churches represent a critical community focal point, especially in underresourced neighborhoods. They are valued and trusted institutions in the community that can quickly mobilize volunteers to help.

Through work with Living Water, I had seen churches play this role in Haiti's 2010 earthquake and the Ebola outbreaks in Liberia and Sierra Leone in 2014 and 2015. I had seen churches play this role in post-genocide Rwanda and in entire regions of Uganda, Nicaragua, and Zambia. Living Water had been building these kinds of partnerships with government, corporate, and nonprofit sector agencies—with churches as the drivers—for years, tangibly displaying the gospel around the globe. As painful as Hurricane Harvey was, there was something special about seeing churches come alive in this way here in Houston. I caught a glimmer in my darkness that God might still be the Master Strategist, calling his church to participate in his redemptive work.

Hurricane Harvey caused $128 billion of property and environmental damage.[12] Trucks would be hauling wreckage out of our city for months to come. Businesses were in ruins. Oil production in the Gulf of Mexico dropped from 1.75 million barrels a day to fewer than 400 thousand. Crude oil tankers were stuck at sea while damaged ports and terminals closed for repair.[13] Refineries shut down operations to direct energies toward controlling the release of hazardous pollutants.[14] A dozen energy facilities burned off gas that had nowhere to go due to infrastructure damage. Nearly half a billion gallons of industrial wastewater mixed with storm water surged from a chemical plant.[15] We would not even know the full extent of the damage for months, if ever.

It struck me how fast life can change. Mile after mile, streets were piled high with the everyday stuff of life—furniture, beds, and toys. Decades of memories had been wiped away in just a few days. None of these people knew what kind of footing their new lives were on. Block after suburban block, toy dolls stared blankly at me from wreckage piled higher than the homes themselves. I thought about how much we humans cling to our things when facing crisis, looking

Figure 4.1. One devastated block in Houston after Hurricane Harvey

to possessions for stability, and how easily things can be pulled out from under us.

Returning my attention to Living Water International, I calculated that we would face an additional $2 million budget shortfall as a result of Harvey. We had already been on soft financial ground before the storm. Historically, half our annual budget came from Houston. Now Houstonians would be overextended just taking care of each other. We would be directing our charitable gifts toward family, friends, and neighbors across town, not across the globe. I turned the numbers over in my head, running scenarios. All of them left Living Water on the rocks.

Our annual fundraising gala was just weeks away. We wondered if we should cancel it. It was hard to imagine asking Houstonians for money in the apocalyptic wasteland our city had become. Then again, it was our biggest fundraising event of the year. We depended on it for our very existence. Every year the gathering of over a thousand supporters raised about $3 million of our $25 million annual budget. That is a lot of money for us. There has never been a year in which Living Water could have made ends meet without our annual gala.

I put the question to our board. I estimated that if we proceeded with the gala, the best we could hope for was about half our normal revenue. The board voted and the results were split 50/50. Half said, "The show must go on." Half said we should cancel it.

Our gala theme that year was "To the Ends of the Earth." A few short weeks before, it had been an inspiring and powerful message about the church offering water and demonstrating and proclaiming the gospel to the ends of the earth. We found layers of meaning in the ways we bear witness to God's love at home in Jerusalem, among our near neighbors in Judea and Samaria, and to our distant neighbors at the ends of the earth. Now it seemed we did not have a stable enough foundation to have such dreams.

Board member Becky Morris sent me a note. She and her husband, Malcolm, had lost their home in the flood. Becky had created a tour experience in our office called "The Story of the Thirsty" that serves church groups and schoolteachers who want to teach kids about the thirsty in other parts of the world. She is easy to spot when we travel abroad together because she is always surrounded by giggling children. At first, I assumed she had written the note because its content was too emotionally overwhelming to tell me in person. As I read, I realized she had written it to clearly present the strength of her conviction:

> Mike, we have got to have this gala. We cannot forget about the thirsty people around the world. Even as we suffer because of too much water, we cannot forget about those who do not have enough. We cannot NOT have this gala.

I had not been able to trust my intuition about the gala, or our board's split vote, but I *could* trust Becky's faith. I announced that we *would* proceed with the gala.

This gave me an opportunity to celebrate Becky's faith, but it did not solve any of my problems. I knew the best we could hope for was half our normal revenue, which would still render us unable to meet our commitments.

Faith is paramount to accomplish our mission. Even when things are going well, it is impossible to anticipate social eruptions in Honduras, mudslides in Sierra Leone, hurricanes in Haiti, cholera outbreaks in Liberia, or famine on the Horn of Africa. It is impossible to anticipate accidents on the road, assaults, earthquakes, or coups. On faith, we build systems with the gifts God has provided, believing in God's sovereign provision, and then trust that he is in control. The trust part is much easier when we can see affirmation that we are carrying out God's will. It is easier to make the gutsy calls when you can see the Creator of the universe in your corner. As a leader, when I feel like my spiritual perspective may be lacking, it seems impossible to make the next call.

In times of doubt, I recall the spiritual insights I had in Senegal thirty years ago:

I am not alone.

God knows me.

God loves me.

There is no need for fear.

God is at work restoring our world.

God invites me to take part in that work.

We are a community.

I can participate in God's work and invite others to do the same.

I had lived my entire adult life on that epiphany, but now doubts haunted me. I had no evidence of God's provision anymore. Worse, I had led hundreds of people around the world to bet their livelihoods on my expressed faith in God's invitation. They had families to support. The thought that I could have led them into crisis based on an illusion filled me with dread. I had built my life on the belief that the Master

Strategist will provide as long as we discern and carry out God's will. I had asked others to do the same. Now it seemed my faith was not deep enough to see our tanking economy, the oil market crash, and Hurricane Harvey's ruins as God's provision. We were relationally stressed at work. My wife had cancer. None of this felt like the provision of a loving God who is involved in our affairs.

I began to consider that maybe I *am* alone, I may *not* be in God's arms, God may *not* be in control, he may *not* be the Master Strategist, inviting us to do his work, providing for us as we discern his will. Perhaps you can imagine how dark and lonely these thoughts were. For a long time now, I had been hearing no answers to my prayers. I felt alone, not just in human terms, but *spiritually* alone. I needed an olive branch. If not a solution, I needed some bit of evidence that there is another shore out there, a sign, just enough to give me the will to keep navigating the ark.

About forty days after Hurricane Harvey hit, I received that olive branch. Early that morning I was tossing and turning in bed. Unable to sleep, I went into my office by myself to pray before dawn. Soon, I was complaining to God:

Why?

Are you still around?

Are you still faithful?

Why did you leave me alone here?

Why did you allow this situation?

Do you still want us to do this work?

I opened my Bible to Acts 1:8 and read the words that inspired our gala theme:

Do not leave Jerusalem, but wait for the gift my Father promised. ... You will receive power when the Holy Spirit comes upon you; and you will be my witnesses in Jerusalem, and in all Judea and Samaria, and to the ends of the earth. (Acts 1:4, 8)

I read that passage, which recorded Christ's instruction about forty days after his death, over and over, meditating on its context, trying to wrap my head around my dilemma. Jesus had been crucified, died, was buried, and had risen. All of this took place in and around Jerusalem. The disciples had lost their dream of Christ overturning the Roman Empire and establishing his kingdom on earth. They likely felt alone, abandoned, and afraid of the future. They didn't fully understand the resurrection yet. Nobody had expected a resurrected messiah.

It was in their moment of weakness, vulnerability, confusion, and doubt that Jesus told his disciples to stay where they were and wait. At their lowest moment, Christ's assurance to his disciples was that they would be given power by the Holy Spirit. With that power, Jesus said, they would be God's witnesses, first *in Jerusalem.*

It occurred to me that morning that for years I had always thought that being able to serve marginalized people at "the ends of the earth" was possible because God had gifted me strength through a solid foundation. God has blessed many of us with education, resources, health, information, churches, and families. I had always assumed that from this solid foundation, we reach out to fragile communities. For decades I would reach out, then come back to my home, church, and office to recharge so I could extend again. I had convinced myself that I receive power from my solid foundation—but that had never really been the case. Jesus' promise to his disciples about the Holy Spirit was given when he knew that they would be weak.

That early morning, I began to consider that the power which comes from God is not the gift of our solid foundation, our personal resources, or our relational networks, but the Holy Spirit. The Holy Spirit came upon the disciples in their despair after they lost their rabbi and to Becky after she lost her home. Even in our weakest moments God's gift is there, waiting to emerge, and give us his power. I still had no solution to my problems, but I knew there was another shore out there. That was my olive branch!

So, I prayed, *what about Living Water? We need help. Houston cannot meet its traditional commitments to the thirsty around the world. What do we do?*

Not audibly, but in my mind, I heard God say, *Go to your near neighbor. Go to Judea and Samaria and ask them to stand in the gap for Houston to be of service to the ends of the earth.*

I recognized the familiar voice of the Master Strategist. Finally, I had something I could *do.* This was strategy. God was speaking to me in my native tongue. I could not see the other shore yet, but I knew it was out there, and the Holy Spirit had given me courage to keep navigating the ark.

I gathered our marketing and communications team and shared the idea of asking "Judea and Samaria" for help. They had a lot on their plates at the moment. They were in the middle of a fall fundraising campaign, the gala they are responsible for was coming up, and they had just lost weeks to the hurricane. I knew they were not looking for extra things to do, but I told them I really thought this was from God. I watched as their faces passed through all the stages of grief: denial, anger, bargaining, sadness, and acceptance, then something more like understanding, maybe enthusiasm, perhaps even hope.

I suggest that it is no coincidence that the dove Noah took as a sign of hope in his hour of need has become a symbol of the Holy Spirit. Whether it is Jesus' disciples in their darkest hour, or me in mine, the gift of God's Holy Spirit is always there, always intervenes . . . and is occasionally visible. I only saw in hindsight how God had me, my wife, and Living Water in his sovereign hand the whole time, which I will share more fully with you in the epilogue.

It was precisely the depth of doubt, which culminated in these first four reflections, that sent me on the soul-searching journey back in time and around the world to produce this book. I pray that the stories in the following reflections might serve as an olive branch for you, evidence that there is another shore out there. The Lord has always guided the church to truly be his witnesses at home in Jerusalem, away in all Judea and Samaria, and even to the ends of the earth—and as it turns out, it is happening in powerful ways virtually everywhere you look, and it can be a great adventure!

Reflect

Remember your own dark night of the soul. Perhaps you are experiencing it now. Where did you turn for help? Where could you turn for help today?

Write

Identify what helped you "see the other shore."

Share

Share your appreciation with someone who helped you out of your dark night. Or share your need for comfort, insight, or power to carry on with someone you trust or with the Lord.

PART TWO

IN JERUSALEM, AND IN ALL JUDEA AND SAMARIA

KNOW THE FAMILY FROM WHICH YOU WERE FORMED

When I was a child,
I talked like a child,
I thought like a child,
I reasoned like a child.
When I became a man,
I put the ways of childhood behind me.

1 CORINTHIANS 13:11

I**N PART ONE,** you joined me in my descent to the dark night of the soul. Perhaps you considered how you view the *advance directive* of Scripture, how to cultivate *love*, endure the tests of your *faith*, and experience the *hope* and power of the Holy Spirit. Part two of this book is my soul-searching journey back in time illustrating how my faith and perspective of the church expanded outward through the concentric contexts of family, community, city, and the world.

Family could be immediate or extended, or perhaps close friends or groups. As we reflect on the families *from* which we were formed, we do so for the purpose of knowing the family *for* which we were formed. As children of God, we are all brothers and sisters in the family we call *the church.*

As you read this story, I invite you to consider your family and the influences in your youth—both positive and negative—that shaped you.

॥॥॥॥॥॥॥॥॥॥॥॥॥॥॥

In the Dutch Reformed cultural tradition in which I grew up, children were taught that their foundation rested on three legs: family, church, and school. Together, these formed a stool that was remarkably sturdy, though not always comfortable. A little three-legged stool can really broaden a kid's horizons. It is easy to forget what it is like to be three feet tall. We forget how the extra foot of a three-legged stool empowers us to reach new heights and see new sights.

The first leg, my family, was led by a stern Dutch immigrant father for whom *family* meant "work." For him, that meant day shifts as a manual laborer, night shifts at the factory, and mowing lawns on weekends. For me, it meant a childhood traded for a spot on my dad's workforce. From the first grade on, every moment I was not in school I was working for my father. I was dutiful, and I worked as hard as I could, but I was not happy about it.

The second leg of my stool was Escalon Christian Reformed Church. The Christian Reformed Church (CRC) is a relatively small, Calvinist congregation formed by Dutch immigrants to North America. At Escalon CRC, we worshiped every Sunday morning, studied the Heidelberg Catechism every Sunday night, and discussed sermons over coffee and cake between the two. As boys, we were members of the Calvinist Cadet Corps. As teens we added Young People's Society on Wednesday evenings to our schedule.

The third leg was Ripon Christian School. All the children of Dutch immigrants in the area where I grew up went to Ripon Christian. I knew the same kids at home, church, and school during all my formative years, and their families looked just like mine.

The three-legged stool on which my childhood faith stood was sturdy and spare, just like everything about being the child of a Dutch immigrant. It gave me identity, structure, meaning, and a clear ethical code that was consistent at home, church, school, and work. It was rigid, and so was I. I had no idea things could be any other way. Like many immigrant groups, Dutch people fleeing from World War II stuck together. Whether in Canada, California, or Argentina, Dutch Reformed churches all look pretty much the same. They all have the same order of worship. They all sing the same psalms and hymns. They have all been studying the same Heidelberg Catechism in the same format of 129 questions and answers in fifty-two weekly sessions per year since 1563. As a child, I never even imagined there was another way to be a Christian.

I did not have a clear image of my father's three-legged stool until he, Natalie, and I went back to the Netherlands together, and he told us about life under Nazi occupation. At the time of our trip, he was seventy-four years old, and it was his first time back since the War. As we walked along the streets of my father's hometown, Andijk (pronounced "on dike," so aptly Dutch), I was struck by how familiar everything was. The names on storefronts and gravestones could have been roll call at Ripon Christian School. The lace curtains on windows and simple home-cooked meals were just like those in every Dutch immigrant home in America.

What seemed different to me was how much life in Europe focused on the past, while we in America seem focused on the future. In Andijk, the "new" church steeple was built hundreds of years ago, and people still recalled the old one. My hometown of Escalon, California was incorporated in 1957, and everyone in it had their sights set on a better future for their children.

With pride, my father showed me his name—Jan Mantel—inscribed on the cornerstone of the home built by his father before the war. He was my Opa's firstborn son, so the home would have been his if not for the Nazi invasion.

"Young Jan!" (pronounced "Yahn") an elderly man shouted. He must have been in his nineties, and he recognized my seventy-four-year-old father as the teen who once helped the Dutch resistance hide people behind a false wall in Opa's barn. They called it "the hiding place," similar to many Dutch Christians who helped their Jewish neighbors escape the Nazi holocaust, as well described by Corrie ten Boom in her book *The Hiding Place*.[1]

In May of 1940 Adolf Hitler gave orders to invade the Netherlands. On the fourth day of that invasion, the Luftwaffe dropped more than a thousand bombs on Holland's second-biggest city, Rotterdam. The bombing caused massive firestorms that overwhelmed the Dutch army, forcing them to surrender the following day. The Nazi occupation began.

When the German military needed more soldiers, it raided homes in occupied territories and forcefully conscripted young men. My father and his brothers built the hiding place behind a false wall in Opa's barn to hide from Nazi soldiers. They made it available to the Dutch resistance and received whomever the resistance brought for safe hiding. Jews, fellow resisters, Allied soldiers, or young men avoiding the Nazi draft would lean their backs against the false wall to make it sound solid as German soldiers banged on it with the butts of their rifles. On one occasion my father watched through a peephole as Nazis held Opa at gunpoint.

"We know you are hiding people in there," they barked. "Do you want to die?"

"You are not looking for anyone here," Opa told them in impeccable German. Everyone who had been hidden in the hiding place agreed that they owed their lives to Opa's flawless German.

As the war intensified, the Nazis demanded ever-more human and material resources from their occupied territories. Poverty grew insufferable as Germany directed the nation's food and fuel to the war, culminating in the *Hongerwinter* of 1944 and 1945. A famine killed tens of thousands and forced 4.5 million people to survive on starvation rations from soup kitchens. My father told me about squeezing oil from grains for fuel and about winters they survived on home-grown turnips and potatoes. Opa turned a bicycle into a generator that powered a single lightbulb. Every night my dad and his brothers took turns pedaling it to illuminate Opa's nightly reading.

The Netherlands in ruins, Jan Mantel set his sights on the New World. For him that meant Australia, Canada, or Argentina. He was anxious to escape to any of them, but he had no money to pay for a voyage across the Atlantic. Opa remembered a Jewish shipper whose son he had sheltered in the hiding place, and he called in a favor. In no time at all, Dad was Canada-bound on a commercial freighter—in the owner's cabin!

Basking in his unfamiliar high-society status, young Jan encountered a beautiful woman among the proletariat in makeshift tents scattered across the deck.

"This is no place for a beautiful woman like you," he said. "Why don't you join me in my cabin?"

Moments later that beautiful woman was at his door . . . *with her husband and children.* Jan spent the rest of the voyage seasick alongside the woman's seasick kids. It wasn't until years later that he met and married my mother, the love of his life, on another trip to America from Canada.

In those days immigration to Canada required that one secure a sponsor who committed to employ the immigrant for one year. When his year of indentured servitude was over, Dad started growing gladiola bulbs, then got a job at a flour mill. Flour is flammable as a fine dust in the air. I was four years old when the flour mill exploded, and my father lost his job.

"I would rather be warm and poor than cold and poor," Dad announced, and we packed our 1954 Buick and a trailer made from the bed of an old pickup truck. Next thing I knew we were bound for sunny California. Some of my first vivid memories are of fighting with my siblings in that Buick, and of Dad's massive hand swiping across its wide back seat, smacking each of us in one swoop.

"Not fair!" we protested.

"Vell, *one* of you is guilty!" Dad shouted back in his heavy Dutch brogue.

When we lost our car keys, my brother, sister, and I watched quietly as our father shattered the ignition with a cinder block. Never delicate, his approach was to smash first and figure things out later. Eventually he did figure out how to hotwire the car, and again we were on our way. When our car lost reverse gear, Dad said we didn't need it because California was in front of us, not behind us. Thanks to our ties in the Dutch immigrant community, a local Dutch family in Escalon, California, offered to take us in and help us get on our feet.

Dad got a job working nights at the Campbell's Soup factory and another raking almonds during the day. After a few months he traded in his almond rake for a position at a landscaping company where his get-it-done approach quickly earned him a position as foreman. As a side-hustle he had a weekend lawn-mowing business, grew it, and went into competition with his former boss.

From age six, I worked for my father every Saturday, holiday, and

Figure 5.1. My mom and dad on the vacation trip on which I would be born

summer day, and I hated it. I wanted to play like other kids. I knew my father as a boss, not as a dad. When he was not acting as our boss, he was away at work. On his birthday we left cards on the counter because we rarely ever saw him in person. He was a hard driver, but we did not complain to him because all the other fathers in our immigrant community worked just as hard with their children.

My mother, Marian, filled the emotional gap for me, my brothers, my sister, and most of our friends. She was always available with a warm welcome, ever-present laughter, and hearty encouragement. Everyone in the neighborhood called her "Ma," and all were eager to receive one of her famous bear hugs. She was one of the most hopeful, faith-filled, and tenacious people I have ever known. She brought love into our world. Ma Mantel was the fierce protector and shrewd champion of all those she loved.

In the sixth grade we moved twelve miles down the road from Escalon to Modesto. In my preteen experience, this represented a huge cultural shift—from Escalon Christian Reformed Church to Modesto Christian Reformed Church. This was an opportunity to reinvent myself.

I had always wanted to be a Cub Scout or Boy Scout, but I was never allowed because it would interfere with work. I was never even allowed to join the Calvinist Cadet Corps, although all of my friends were members. The Cadets were like the Boy Scouts for Christian Reformed Church boys; girls joined Calvinettes (now called GEMS).[2] I saw our move as a window of opportunity.

"Dad, now that we're at a new church, can I become a Cadet?"

I was shocked when he agreed. I hit the ground running, as though Dad's permission would soon expire. I earned every badge, patch, trophy, and honor the Calvinist Cadet Corps offered. I loved everything about being a Cadet. I loved the uniforms, merit badges, soap box derbies, and camporees. I loved tying knots, starting fires, and gathering around the fake campfire in the social hall as we closed out our meetings singing our theme song, "Living for Jesus":

Living for Jesus a life that is true,
Striving to please Him in all that I do;
Yielding allegiance, glad-hearted and free,
This is the pathway of blessing for me!

Pathway of blessing was an understatement. Suddenly, I had the attention of the men at our church who had the most spectacular interests. They taught me about archery, backpacking, camping, and all kinds of things for which my father never had time. It was my first learning experience outside of family, school, or church services, and I went bonkers. In two years, I advanced from Recruit to Pathfinder, Builder, Left Star Guide, Right Star Guide, and Advanced Guide, winning every soap box derby along the way. The Calvinist Cadet Corps' highest honor, Servant Leader, now requires eleven merit badges on the road from recruit to advanced guide. I earned twenty-seven. Some kids took eight years to earn that many, but I was on fire. Axemanship, Bible Exploration, Camp Cooking, Calvinism—I covered myself in merit badges and was named Cadet of the Year. My Cadet counselor later told me I was the most serious kid he had ever met.

Faith was also a very serious matter for me. I was absolutely convinced that God was watching me day and night. I believed that all life's questions were answered in the Bible and the Heidelberg Catechism, and I had complete faith in the elders and deacons at church. I was obsessed with religion. When it seemed to me that others were not so serious about their faith, I grew concerned that God would punish them. It was all spelled out in "Question & Answer 10" of the Heidelberg Catechism:

Q. Does God permit such disobedience and rebellion to go unpunished?

A. Certainly not. God is terribly angry with the sin we are born with as well as the sins we personally commit. As a just judge, God will punish them both now and in eternity, having declared:

"Cursed is everyone who does not observe and obey all the things written in the book of the law."

In case there was any doubt, the Catechism footnoted a string of verses to support its answer.[3] As a young, serious student, I fixated on

Q&A 10 without taking into consideration the larger context of God's grace and redemption. I remember praying to God, telling him I did not want to be so serious anymore. I was on a job site at the time, feeling the weight of it all, and stopped pushing a lawnmower to pray. With my palms facing up to heaven I begged him to lighten my load and told him I just wanted to be a kid.

If it was not the weight of our eternal destiny causing me grief, it was my big ears. From kindergarten through fifth grade, older kids on the school bus flicked my big ears, and it infuriated me. Now that we had moved, though, I considered that maybe my life was about to change. On the first day of sixth grade, I boarded my new school bus with peace in my heart. *Finally,* I thought, *a new city, a new bus—nobody is going to flick my ears!*

Utterly unaware that I had six years of built-up ear-flicking rage coursing through my veins, some unfortunate kid flicked my ear, and I decked him. I knew Jesus did not approve of that punch, but I was impressed with how quickly it solved my problem. Life was presenting all kinds of opportunities to reinvent myself, so I began to think about the big one.

"Who defines 'popular'?" I asked my friend Billy. Popularity was the coin of the middle school realm, and I had not enjoyed a cent of it. I was bashful, a loner, more serious than other kids, and obsessed with religion. None of these were ingredients for popularity. Sixth grade was the perfect time to make a change.

"Why don't we just decide that *we* are popular?" I asked Billy. We made a pact then and there that we would become popular. We defined ourselves as the center of the universe, visualized our future as popular kids, and started taking steps to embody our vision. In a few months, we were "lead dogs" in the sixth grade.

As I entered high school, I decided that I would get off to yet another good start by committing not to tolerate abuse from anyone. I decided that if an upper classman picked on me, he would get decked like an ear-flicker on a middle school bus. My attitude as a freshman defied the high school pecking order, which made me a target for upper classmen who wanted to put me in my place. During lunch they would pour orange juice in my hair, pick me up and drop me down on my knees in front of them, beat me up, and embarrass me. The next day in gym class, I would target one of the bullies while he was alone and go after him. This became my routine. For two whole years I got beat up at lunch, then sought revenge the following day at the gym. This may not have been the cleverest plan. I recognize now the same approach my father used when smashing the dash of our 1954 Buick with a cinder block. The only reason the plan seemed to work was that I eventually outgrew my bullies. I am friends with some of them now, but at the time we were locked in a cycle of attacks and counter-attacks. Although not the quickest route to peace, enduring that daily hazing built a tenacity that I would use for the rest of my life. And Billy and I were popular.

My popularity status was only one change during that fateful sixth-grade year when we moved from Escalon to Modesto. In terms of my childhood faith, nothing so broadened my horizons as my new friendship with Juan Carlos and his friend Art. At the age of twelve, Juan and Art were the first people to sneak me out of my Christian Reformed Church culture for adventures that exposed me to other worlds.

Everyone I had ever known at home, church, or school was from a Dutch immigrant family just like mine. Juan's Spanish-speaking Cuban Catholic family may as well have been from another planet. Art went to a Black Pentecostal church. The world, I learned, was a lot bigger than my elders had been telling me.

Juan, Art, and I used to call one another's parents to ask what was for dinner, then show up together at the home with the most promising menu. I had previously thought everyone ate plain boiled potatoes and meat just like we did, but apparently the rest of the world was frying food in oil and slathering it with spices, condiments, and sauces.

At Juan's home we ate tostones, empanadas, or *ropa vieja,* which was shredded beef, slow cooked with onions, garlic, peppers, and wine. If we chose to eat at my house, it was likely because everyone needed a good dose of my mother's humor, not her cooking. By comparison, it was still the *Hongerwinter* at the Mantel house with our boiled turnips and potatoes.

I began to realize that there was more to the world than what I could see from my three-legged stool. I had been such a serious working kid for such a long time. I was starting to wake up to the suspicion that there is more to life than work and religion, and I felt like I needed a change. Juan and Art were not preoccupied with religion at all. They were playing football, chasing girls, and inviting me to join them on grand adventures. Juan was a black belt in Taekwondo and a ladies' man. We used to have conversations about whether it is better to commit to a deep relationship with just one girl or to date widely. I said deep. Juan said wide.

It made a very big impression on me that Juan's grandparents lived with him. I admired his family's respect for elders and the role Juan's grandparents played in his life. Spanish was the primary language in their home, so I did not understand their words, but I saw them physically display affection in ways my family never did. The love I saw expressed in their home and their care for the older generation positively shaped how I wanted to be with my own family in ways that our Dutch community had not taught. Seeing three generations under one roof in their home likely played a role in Natalie's and my decision to invite my father and later Natalie's mother to live with us.

When Dutch Christian Reformed kids reached high school, we started going to additional catechism classes and Young People's Society on Wednesday nights. These church activities seemed less enticing to me after Juan and Art introduced me to new social horizons. We had gone over the Catechism in its entirety every year of our lives. The Calvinist Cadet Corps offered some adventure and novelty for a while, but then adolescence began to present new forms of adventure. Other teens at Young People's Society felt the same and started sneaking away to smoke, drink, or do other things that made us feel like we made our own rules. In the Christian Reformed Church, we affirm the faith of our infant baptism just before becoming adults. According to our tradition, an all-knowing and sovereign God elected us into faith at the world's foundation. At baptism, we seal the covenant between God and his children. On the verge of adulthood, we profess our own commitment to that covenant before setting out into the world.

On schedule, I sat with the elders of our church, and they interrogated me about the Catechism, theology, and my beliefs. I told them what they wanted to hear, but my heart was not in it. I no longer felt like these guys knew the answers to all life's questions. I was not even sure I believed in God anymore. I went through it all as a formality, so as not to cause a stir in my family or church. I professed my faith out loud in front of the whole congregation, then continued to take a series of small steps away from the three-legged stool of my childhood.

I started going out to parties, drinking, and having fun like other teenagers. I was done with the guilt-ridden, restrictive lifestyle of my younger years. I did not want to have a debate about what the Catechism called my "depraved nature," or "evil inclinations." The Heidelberg Catechism had taught me that I, like all descendants of Adam and Eve, was "inclined to all evil" and "totally unable to do any good."[4] I had no desire to argue about the catechism or its interpretation of Scripture. I just wanted to be normal and have fun like everyone else. However, our closed culture interpreted that as sin and did not encourage discussion. There was no middle ground to be found and no conversation to be had.

"When I was a child," Paul wrote to the Corinthians, "I talked like a child, I thought like a child, I reasoned like a child. When I became a man, I put the ways of childhood behind me" (1 Corinthians 13:11).

I did not put the ways of childhood behind me in quite the way the apostle Paul would have wanted me to. Then again, neither did Paul.

He spent a fair amount of time persecuting Christians before the Holy Spirit changed his life and, through him, changed the world. It would still be quite a while before I would have my own "road to Damascus" experience. Until then, putting the ways of childhood behind me meant kicking my three-legged stool aside and wandering through darkness for a time. Doing so was sometimes fun and sometimes very painful. For a time I lost sight of God altogether, but in his mercy, God never lost sight of me.

Today I am grateful for the solid three-legged stool of family, church, and school that supported my childhood faith. These influences shaped me. I rebelled against them before eventually embracing them again. Whatever flaws my stool had, I feel grateful for the institutions and community that formed me—immigrant work ethic, Heidelberg Catechism, boiled turnips, and all.

Reflecting on the origin story of my Christian faith from the vantage point of middle age helped me understand where I come from, who I am, whose I am, and how God prepares us for service in the family of all sons and daughters of God, who we seek to serve at home and among neighbors near and far, even to the ends of the earth.

Reflect

Reflect on what it means to you to be a part of your family, then reflect on what it means to you to be a part of God's family. In your view, what is the relationship between the two?

Write

However pleasant or unpleasant your early life may have been, write down the three things you most value from your upbringing.

Share

Share with someone you trust a couple of things you dearly value and one thing that you would ask God to redeem in your life.

CHRIST'S COMMUNITY SPANS FAITH TRADITIONS

For just as each of us has one body with many members,
and these members do not all have the same function,
so in Christ we, though many, form one body,
and each member belongs to all the others.
We have different gifts, according
to the grace given to each of us.

ROMANS 12:4-6

WHEN I WAS A CHILD, it was still possible to grow up in relative social isolation, believing that my church doctrine was the *only* form of Christianity. I was almost a teenager before my friendship with Juan Carlos and Art showed me that other kinds of Christians even existed. In my little Dutch immigrant world, long before the invention of the internet, with only one newspaper and three television channels, I had very little awareness of people outside of my physical world.

That isolated world of my childhood is gone forever. Today, through social media, every person on earth with access to the internet is instantly connected through millions of channels and is intimately aware of people unlike themselves.

Faced with the reality of denominational diversity, some people hunker down and defend the truth of their tradition against all others. Others choose to loosen their doctrinal grip for pragmatic reasons. Some throw in the towel on the church completely, while others find a path to learn from each other's differences without losing their distinctiveness.

By some estimates Christians are now divided into more than 33,000 denominations, with many engaging in arguments about politics, atonement theories, end-times interpretations, and social issues.[1] While many of these debates help us refine our own personal and community perspectives on important issues, to focus on our disagreements erodes our ability to work together on significant global issues. Many of our young people no longer find the debates inspiring, and some are leaving the church instead of participating.

Given the personal turmoil in my own inner life and my choice for autonomy, my reaction was to stop believing in God altogether, only to return to faith seven painful years later. The next concentric ring of my expanding faith journey offered worthwhile lessons that came through struggle and pain. It got ugly for a while, which you will soon see as a selfish and embarrassing version of young me emerges from under a pile of empty beer bottles. But my story does not end there.

As you read this story, I invite you to consider people that you know from outside of your faith tradition. How do you interact with them?

<hr>

I had one pair of jeans, two white shirts, no money, and I was living on a borrowed couch. I was having trouble sleeping in those days because I no longer believed in God, yet I somehow believed that this God I did not believe in would punish me for my disbelief.

I was in my early twenties. I should have been in the best shape of my life, but my health was rotten. My ankle was either fractured or sprained, swollen to the size of a grapefruit, but I had no money to see a doctor.

My brother Pete came over, saw me in my pathetic state, and gathered all the empty beer bottles scattered about. He returned those bottles to the grocery store to collect the ten-cent deposit on each, then used that money to rent a pair of crutches for me.

Covered in sweat, I sat up in my borrowed couch and reached for my crutches rented with beer bottle money. I felt winded at the mere thought of standing up. My ankle throbbed with every heartbeat, and it hurt even more when I lowered it to the floor. I had no incentive to get off that couch. I had no job. Nobody would lend me money. I was just 190 pounds of self-indulgent loser, wondering how I ended up like this.

The borrowed couch I slept on belonged to the only daughter of a famous Christian preacher, the Reverend Juan Boonstra. He was the voice of *The Back to God Hour*, a radio broadcast on four hundred stations in South and Central America. His daughter, Natalie "Annie" Boonstra, had somehow fallen for me, and I knew he would have been as disgusted with the sight of me as I was.

"When are you going to go live with that Word of God community?" Annie asked. I understood her question to mean she wanted me out of her apartment. I thought she was dumping me, and who could blame her? It was time to reevaluate my life.

My high school adventures with Juan Carlos and Art had been like sneaking out the window of my Christian Reformed Church to gather intelligence about the real world. On those reconnaissance missions, I gained intelligence I had to keep confidential from my friends at Young People's Society at church. I had no place to process my transition into the wider world. My church provided no counseling. We were just supposed to do the right thing. I had nobody to talk to about my compulsion *not* to do the right thing. I did not even know what to make of other Christian denominations. Defending our Calvinist doctrine no longer felt important to me. I felt cut off from my community. I had not been given a bigger container in which my faith could exist alongside that of others. God made no sense to me anymore, so I denied he even existed. Then my religious conditioning led me to feel judged by that God in whom I no longer believed. The pain of that cognitive dissonance led me to self-medicate.

If you know anything about Dutch immigrants or the Christian Reformed Church, you may have already guessed that I made my way to Calvin College in Grand Rapids, Michigan. Our school motto was "My heart I offer to you, Lord, promptly and sincerely." Nothing could have been more precisely designed to compound my faith crisis. There was nothing sincere about my faith. I did not feel inclined to offer my heart to the Lord or anyone else. I no longer bothered with going to church. I was making one bad decision after another, each of them driving me further from God. This dark and self-serving time would go on for about seven years.

My last year of college finally gave me an opportunity to step away from the darkness I had created around myself. I went to Spain for a semester to fulfill a language requirement I had been avoiding. It was an exciting leap into a world I had only glimpsed through my friendship with Juan Carlos. My time in Spain pulled me out of the unhealthy community in which I had embedded myself and gave me a new perspective on life. My new community in Spain drank alcohol but did not get drunk. They played a ball game called *frontón*, and nobody got into fights. They went to bullfights and did wild and exciting things without being self-destructive. My time in Spain gave me a chance to reflect and think about growing up. One of the things I thought a lot about was who I should remove from my life and who I should keep.

Annie Boonstra was at the top of my list of "keepers," so I started writing letters to her. She had been part of my circle of friends for years. I liked her because she could eat as much as me, drink as much as me, and she loved to debate philosophy and theology into the wee hours of the morning. My time in Spain opened my eyes to the fact that I wanted her to be part of my life. When I got home, I asked her out on a date, and she said yes.

One night on top of my little apartment above a thrift store in Grand Rapids, Annie and I got into a discussion about life. I told her I believed that there were only two tracks in life. The first is to make your own law. I quoted the French novelist Honoré de Balzac: "Behind every great fortune lies a great crime," and I said that if you look around, you will find that most everyone with wealth and power got it through some amoral means. The other path is the one I called "the way of the immigrant." You move to America, work with your hands, your kids go to college, they get a better job, then *their* kids go to a better college, and they get an even better job. It was the slow, multigenerational path to a "white picket fence."

I told Annie I intended to take the fast, amoral route to wealth and power, not the slow, multigenerational path to mediocrity, and in that moment the strangest thing happened.

"Annie," I said, leaning over to her, "I just had a thought that was not my thought."

"What do you mean it was not your thought?" she asked.

"It just appeared in my head fully formed," I said. "I don't feel like it was mine, but the thought that appeared was, *Those who serve God do not have to make this choice.*"

"That's a funny thought for a guy who doesn't believe in God," she said.

"I know! I have no idea why I would have thought that."

"So, what are you going to do?" she asked.

"I guess before I choose which path to take, I should figure out whether or not God exists."

"How are you going to do that?"

I told her that I did not know if God existed, but I knew of people who believe he does. I told her about a recent visit with my brother Corey, who was living with a group of "monks in the marketplace" and who had never judged me and always embraced me. Corey lived in an ecumenical charismatic community of about three thousand people in Ann Arbor, Michigan called the Word of God community. Every morning the men in Corey's house woke up at 5:00 a.m., faced a wall, prayed, bowed, and sang with all their hearts. They were really into it. It was next-level stuff, way beyond being an elder at church or anything I had ever seen.

After that conversation, I quickly turned to avoiding visiting the Word of God community. I moved to different places, got different jobs, tried to get loans to do this or that, and everything I did failed. Eventually I ended up back in Grand Rapids on Annie's couch with no place to go, falling into old habits.

One night, Annie and I were walking home together through the snow after a party. I had drunk way too much, and she was getting tired of my antics. She asked me a question that was serious, but in my inebriated state I thought was hilarious.

"Are you trying to put as much evil as you can inside of you before you go to Ann Arbor?"

I laughed at her question, and as I laughed my left foot got stuck in the snow and the right one slipped on the ice, turning me around. My ankle cracked, and in no time at all it had swollen to the size of a grapefruit. Annie got me home, and that was where I woke up covered in sweat on my borrowed couch, reaching for the crutches my brother Pete rented with beer bottle money.

"*When* are you going to go live with that Word of God community in Ann Arbor?" Annie asked.

I would later learn that she had been praying for my soul all along, and she was trying to hasten my search for God. In the moment, though, I thought she was kicking me out of her apartment.

"I'll go on Thursday," I said, and as I said those words, I heard a crack in my ankle and felt it set into place. "Check this out!" I shouted, "I can move my ankle!"

"That's pretty strange," Annie said.

To this day, I do not know if that was coincidence, or psychosomatic, or something else, but in the moment, it really meant something to me. I felt like God was talking to me. The following Thursday, on my twenty-fourth birthday, I got a ride to Ann Arbor where these monk-type guys who were living single for the Lord took me in. They had taken vows of simplicity, chastity, and obedience, which seemed bizarre to me, but I took it as evidence that they were serious. They gave me a private bedroom with a bed while they all slept on the floor in sleeping bags. I had no money, but they fed me and even gave me a $10 a month allowance. All their love and kindness made me feel like they were up to something sneaky.

I told Andy Williamson, the head of the household, that I was there to find out whether God exists. I told him God had a month to reveal himself to me, but this revelation could not happen next weekend because I needed to help Annie Boonstra move from Calvin College back to Chicago.

"We have something coming up this weekend called the Life in the Spirit Seminar," Andy told me, "It's a two-day event, and I really think you need to attend."

"Oh, sorry, that's the weekend I'm helping Annie move. I told you that when I got here."

"Tell me again," Andy said, "why are you here?"

"Because I want to know if God exists," I said.

"Well then, you have a choice to make," Andy said.

I was so mad I felt steam rise from my head. My options in life had become so narrow that a chaste, impoverished, floor-sleeping monk was telling me what to do and where to be. I thought my integrity was more complex than Andy seemed to see.

Annie got worried when I told her I could not help her move. She was a normal, sane, Christian Reformed person just like I had been before I walked away from it all. She knew I was hanging out with these radical, crazy Jesus people. It made no sense to her that I could not just break away to help her move. She considered that maybe some kind of brainwashing was going on, but she was willing to take a wait-and-see posture.

On the first day of the Life in the Spirit Seminar, we went through the Old Testament, looking at the times God called someone into his service. Every time, whether it was Abraham, Moses, the Judges, or the Prophets, God sent them his Holy Spirit to give them power. I knew all that, even though I had not read about it in years. I was comfortable with all those Old Testament stories, but the next day they were going to talk about the New Testament, and I was suspicious. I thought they had used all that Old Testament stuff as a sneaky way to soften me up, then hit me with a bunch of weird New Testament Holy Spirit mumbo-jumbo. I was pretty sure they were going to try to get me to speak in tongues, handle snakes, and who knows what else.

About halfway into the day, they started talking about God sending the power of his Holy Spirit on Pentecost, giving people the power to heal the sick, preach the gospel, have courage, and be God's witnesses in Jerusalem, in Judea and Samaria, and to the ends of the earth. It was actually pretty stirring. I was sufficiently moved to go off to the side of the room by myself and say a very conditional sinner's prayer:

"Dear God," I prayed, "*if* you exist, and *if* you do actually have a Holy Spirit, and *if* your Holy Spirit really does have the power to equip us to obey you, *then* . . . I want that Holy Spirit."

With my eyes still closed, I found myself confessing the sin of the day, the sin of the week, the sin of the month, and the sin of the year. As I prayed, I felt my head physically rise. Every time I felt my head rise, I forced it back down because I was afraid of God. Then I would feel my head rise again, and again I would force it down. It occurred to me how extraordinary this all was, and I thought, *I'm having some kind of religious experience here—this is crazy!*

As I had this experience, I was at the same time judging it as not being real. I must have looked like I was having quite a challenge because someone grabbed my shoulder.

"We'd like to pray with you," he said.

I was not used to men touching me. Judging by the look on his face, I must have reacted like he flicked my ear on a middle school bus.

"What would you like prayer for?" he asked.

"I want to know if God exists," I answered. "And I want to be able to love. I don't think I feel love."

"Alright," he said simply, and people put their hands on me and prayed that I would know that God exists and that I would be able to feel love.

I got up, walked into the bathroom, closed the door, and started bawling. As I cried, I heard a voice in my head say, *Welcome home. Welcome home.*

That night when I went to bed, I was not afraid for the first time in years. I just went to sleep without a worry and felt light when I woke in the morning. Suddenly, I experienced life differently. I had a huge thirst to study the Bible again, only now there were scholars from many Christian traditions all around from whom I could learn. I quit smoking cigarettes so my voice would better contribute to the songs we sang together. I felt this warm lightness of being and fell asleep every night with ease. This went on for about ten days, until one morning when I woke up and I did not feel that warmth and light. It scared me. I was afraid that I had just had a religious experience, and now it was over. I thought God had abandoned me and the fear would again set in.

Oh, Lord, I prayed, *please don't let this be a lie. Please tell me how to do this.*

Life had become so peculiar I no longer knew what was possible. Should I expect another miracle?

I went downstairs where the guys were talking about a passage from Ephesians. I heard in their discussion things I needed to hear, things that answered my questions. There were no more uncanny miracles. Or perhaps the miracle I needed was the provision of a spiritual family. We all had varied backgrounds, experiences, and beliefs, but we did not focus on our differences. We focused on helping one another live a Christ-centered life in practical ways, whatever that meant for each of us.

I invited Annie Boonstra to meet my new community. Her Calvinist, Dutch-Argentine father was not keen on the idea of Annie slipping from her own three-legged stool, but he was confident in God's faithfulness and secure in the knowledge that he and Annie's mother had raised an intelligent and strong woman who would make informed decisions. Also, he was aware that the son of his colleague at *The Back to God Hour*'s Chinese ministry, Calvin Jen, and his wife, Karen, were leaders in the community, lending it a bit of credibility—perhaps we would be in good hands after all. In time, I asked Annie to marry me. In the meantime, as she emerged into her adult life, she had begun to use her proper first name, Natalie, so she became Natalie Mantel. Natalie and I lived in the Word of God community for the next eight years. Cal and Karen became mentors and dear friends to Natalie and me while they modeled for us a beautiful marriage, taught us how to raise children, and invested in our professional development.

Word of God was a community of a few thousand people from all different Christian backgrounds. Most went to their own church every Sunday morning, then gathered with our community on Sunday and Wednesday nights. We had a governance structure, elders, and small groups of all kinds. We gathered in community groups, family groups, men's, women's, and accountability groups, and shared our problems and learned from one another. There were authors in the community to listen to, classes to take, and books we read in groups. We played in the same sports leagues and found all kinds of ways to live life together. There were the Servants of the Word who had chosen to remain single, chaste, and poor; and there were people like us who wanted a family. Some shared homes communally. Others lived as nuclear families and gathered in other ways. We were all one, though we had different styles of relating to God and even different beliefs. Some, but not all of us, believed in healing miracles. People gathered for prayer and healing while the more hesitant members of the community sat in the bleachers and watched.

Figure 6.1. We gathered in community to share and learn from one another

Though our beliefs varied, we were encouraged to keep sight of the fact that we were sisters and brothers who deserved one another's love and respect. Our diversity made us stronger as we found ways to live and worship together in the spirit of the crowd of Africans, Arabs, Asians, Parthians, Medes, Elamites, and people from every nation under heaven in the story of Christian Pentecost (see Acts 2:7-11).

We achieved this unity through three main areas of focus: commitment to community, focus on what we had in common, and the application of biblical principles to our life together. Each of these deserves a moment of reflection, as each has value for the global church today.

Commitment to community. There simply is no community without commitment. In my very first week at Word of God, Andy expected me to commit to the Life in the Spirit Seminar. It annoyed me at the time, but in truth I *did* have a choice to make. As it turned out, choosing a relationship with God became foundational to all my relationships, including my friendship with Annie Boonstra. Had I chosen to honor her request to help her move over my promise to pursue the existence of God, she probably never would have become Natalie Mantel. This was a first step in understanding that commitment requires sacrifice.

Our commitment to one another is the practice of our commitment to God. Every one of us at Word of God was expected to commit to a small group of people and show up for them every time whether we wanted to or not. We committed to listening to what others had to say and share what we had to say. We committed to reading books, taking classes, and learning together. Each of us was also expected to commit to some form of service. Some served by taking on leadership roles. For others, service meant something as simple as helping with setup and take down for community events. Some were called to service on a global level, and others to service that was very local. We helped each other along, whatever service role we chose. Commitment to others is faith in action, and it is essential for building community. And counterintuitively, we learned, serving others leads to less loneliness and increased feelings of purpose, reward, and gratitude, all of which correlate with happiness.

Focus on what we have in common. At Word of God, when we were together, we focused on the core tenets of the Christian faith, and we learned from one another's traditions without compromising our own. We chose to learn from our differences rather than to argue about them. We did not criticize our Catholic friends about transubstantiation, the papacy, or veneration of the Virgin Mary. Neither did anyone challenge John Calvin's controversial doctrine of election. Some people spoke in tongues, but not everybody did. Some of us baptized infants, others baptized professing believers.

Focusing on disagreements is useful for building cohesion within small tribal groups but counterproductive in the interconnected global civilization emerging in the world today. The world will never run out of things to disagree about. Arguing almost never results in the other side saying, "Oh, now I see the light." The real light shines through our love, unity, and service. Over time, our common life in the Word of God was enriched through our diversity.

It wasn't intended that we would all eventually believe the same thing but that from within our own traditions, we would respond to Jesus' call for unity around basic Christian tenets. Our focus on what unified us allowed us to build on the various waves of spiritual development that swept through our diverse traditions without losing our distinctiveness. When people in the Catholic Charismatic Renewal learned something that honored God and built community, we learned it too. When our Messianic Jewish friend unpacked a deep theological or cultural insight, we listened to it. He taught us to adapt beautiful Jewish traditions for application within a Christian body. We learned how to celebrate Seder on Passover, and we developed Christmas and Easter litanies in which everyone had a part. We still use these litanies in my family today. We would never have enjoyed these rich blessings if we had chosen to focus on our differences rather than what we had in common.

Practical application of biblical principles. My family, church, and school provided no shortage of doctrinal principles, but the Word of God community taught me how to *apply* in my everyday life the biblical principles embraced across denominations—to express our faith in action. For example, we agreed that Matthew 18:15-17 would be our model for resolving conflict, and at all levels of leadership and membership, we were directed to intentionally practice using the model. We sought to resolve disputes one-on-one in person first, then if that did not work, addressed the matter in the company of one or two others, then brought it before our elders if necessary. We had courses for applying biblical principles to our relationships, families, community, businesses, and every other aspect of life. We were daily held accountable to exercise prayer, repentance, reconciliation, and countless other real-world applications.

Over the years, I have seen people apply these principles in cultures all around the world. We incorporate them into our approach at Living Water International to bring people together. In some parts of the world when we apply these principles, we see that Christians and Muslims can prioritize the good of their community over their religious differences and work together. In others, it's quite a challenge to get Christians of different denominations to talk to each other. In rural Nicaragua, for example, people often speak as though there are only two world religions: "Christian" and "Catholic"—and the two don't mix. When we started working in Guastomate Community in southern Nicaragua, we recruited Christians from both Protestant and Catholic churches, as well as people from no church at all. It soon became evident that the two religious camps had a contentious history, but we did not focus on that. Instead, we invited them to our Servant-Leader Workshop, where they learned about Jesus as a model for community service. This got them focused on all three principles: their commitment to community in imitation of Jesus, a focus on what they have in common, which was faith in Jesus, and the application of biblical principles, which was the core message of the workshop. We took the same approach as we followed up by inviting them to the workshop Integral Mission of the Church, then more: Community Response; Sanitation and Hygiene; and our Bible Storying Workshop, where they learned how to share their faith through stories and questions.

The lessons they learned served their churches and helped them develop relationships. Next thing they knew, Catholic and evangelical leaders were working together to form their community's first Potable Water and Sanitation Committee. This committee would go on to be recognized by their municipal government and by Nicaragua's National Institute of Water. When they engaged Living Water to drill a water well, they worked together to make a dream come true, and the whole community noticed. In fact, their unity inspired the whole community to contribute to their work financially. This community-wide unity inspired their mayor's office to engage experts to help them plan and build a water tank, water tower, and water distribution system. After years of bickering, both churches learned that it is folly to make themselves feel big by making the other feel small. More importantly, they learned that by committing to their community, focusing on what they have in common, and applying biblical principles to life, both of their churches could grow in ways they had not previously imagined.

Another example of these principles in action comes from West Africa. According to the Pew-Templeton Global Religious Futures Project, Sierra Leone's population is about 78 percent Muslim and 21 percent Christian. One day we were teaching a WASH (Water, Sanitation, and Hygiene) training for pastors there, and a sixty-five-year-old woman who called herself Mammie Hope told us of the desperate need for water at a school she founded. Her backstory was fascinating.

Born with the name Kuria Korma, she was one of many displaced by Sierra Leone's brutal 1999 civil war. She lost two children during that war. Those wartime years saw the most extreme atrocities: the mass rape and murder of civilians; the abduction, drugging, and brainwashing of child soldiers; and intimidation tactics that included hacking off civilians' hands with machetes and even eating them.[2] The stress was too much for Kuria's marriage. Her husband abandoned her, leaving her to raise their surviving children alone.

As a devout Muslim, Kuria Korma sincerely believed that her faith brought her closer to God. One day as an elderly woman in her new post-war community told her about Jesus, she sensed that something was missing in her spiritual life. It was a difficult decision, but she decided to follow Jesus. "I said to myself," she shared, "'if it pleases God to draw me to himself, then that was a decision worth making.'" She and her four surviving children were baptized at the Deeper Life Bible Church. Having found hope in Jesus, she changed her name to Mammie Hope, the name everyone knows her by today.

In 2010, Mammie Hope heard God tell her to start a school. God's request sounded absurd to her. She was not even educated herself, and she had a hard time taking care of her own children. Yet she had faith that God had called her to demonstrate her commitment to community, so she founded Hope Preparatory Primary and Junior Secondary School to serve all her neighbors, focusing on what they had in common, which was a need for education. Applying biblical principles, she not only responded to God's call herself, but soon also began to notice God touching other people, inspiring them to offer financial, spiritual, and physical support. But she still had problems. The community council closed the school several times due to health complications caused by their lack of drinking water. With no school fees being collected, school managers got into debt with microfinance lenders. Not knowing what to do next, they prayed.

As God would have it, a church on the other side of the world was also praying, asking God for an opportunity to be his witnesses to the ends of the earth. In God's plan as Master Strategist, these prayers brought us together at that WASH seminar where Mammie Hope asked for help. Living Water International drilled a water well at her school, constructed sanitation facilities, and trained students and teachers in good hygiene practices. In this healthy new school environment, enrollment increased, the school got out of debt, and now they have new hope.

Zoom out, and you will see a piece of the macrostory of how God is weaving together his people to act in Nicaragua, Sierra Leone, and the United States as they commit to their own community, focus on what they have in common (whether in our own neighborhoods or our global community), and apply biblical principles at home, among near neighbors, and even to the ends of the earth.

Natalie and I never saw the Word of God community as our final destination but as a place to learn lessons that we would apply later wherever God would lead us. In fact, it was through relationships we built at Word of God that I ended up working for Tom Monaghan at Domino's Farms and eventually ended up in Senegal having the spiritual insight that changed my life. The friends we made at Word of God stretched our thinking and extended our practice beyond our local church. Embracing our denominational diversity enriched our lives, but perhaps most importantly, the experience opened our eyes to the vast nature of the body of Christ.

From global pandemics to interlinked economies to emerging new social media networks, every passing year reveals in new ways how interconnected the human family is. Christians were given a foundational image of unity in diversity in the story of Pentecost, foreshadowed by Christ's own prayer for oneness on his darkest night. Because of this image, Christians are uniquely equipped to lead the way in demonstrating unity in the midst our diversity, and we can do so without letting go of any of our core beliefs.

Reflect

Reflect on the extent to which you have, or have not, interacted with people of faith traditions other than your own.

Write

Write a list of things you could learn from people of a faith tradition other than your own.

Share

Share one thing from the above list with someone from another faith tradition and ask him or her to tell you more about it.

THE WORLD EXISTS IN THE CITY

There is neither Jew nor Gentile, neither slave nor free,
nor is there male and female, for you are all one in Christ Jesus.

GALATIANS 3:28

WHETHER ON A metropolitan scale or a global one, many of us struggle to understand the dynamics of wealth, power, and justice that influence our lives.

As my concentric circles of influence began to expand, my awareness of these dynamics began to expand. In this reflection, you will follow me into a world of seemingly unlimited opportunities of wealth, then into an impoverished community in West Africa, then into a job with one of the world's largest Christian relief and development organizations. Dynamics between classes, ethnicities, and religions became tangible obstacles to achieving ministry goals in ways I had not expected. I learned some very important lessons from some of the most inspiring people you could ever hope to meet: from a Vietnamese man named Lộc Lê Châu to Dr. Lincoln Scott on the rough West Side of Chicago.

As you read this story, consider the lines that divide people in your city or the one nearest you—wealth, poverty, ethnicity, denomination, gender—what are the "hot buttons" that affect your neighbors?

⸻

For the last thirty years, I have lived in Chicago and Houston, but I was not always a big city guy. As a teenager working for my dad, I had wanted just two things out of life: air-conditioning and a chance to meet the women who worked in the magical refrigerated offices that contained my dad's customers.

My family and friends all agreed that I was not college material. I considered that maybe they were right, but I saw no other path to air-conditioning and a mixed gender workplace, so after a year at Modesto Junior College, I enrolled in Calvin College. I chose business economics as my degree because that seemed to be the path to acquiring the wealth my parents never had.

After college, my first shot out of the gate was a job as an accounts payable clerk at a sound reinforcement company. I knew almost nothing about accounting, and I could not type, so generating checks was painstaking. I faked it every day, and I was miserable. I hated the idea of being a salesman, but I was so desperate to get out of that office, I took a job selling the Data General One briefcase computer. The nine-pound, battery-powered computer sported 128Kb of RAM, dual 3½-inch disk drives, and an LCD screen that displayed a whopping twenty-five lines at once, a breakthrough at the time.

Later, a PhD computer guy at the Domino's distribution company told me the computer age had only just begun.

"There will come a day when all the computers in the world will talk to each other," he said.

I told him he'd lost his mind. I had been a cutting-edge briefcase computer salesman. Natalie and I were married by then, and she was trained on the newest personal computers at a large accounting firm, so I knew a thing or two about computers.

"Right now, the US military is developing something called 'the internet,'" he claimed. "All computers will be able to connect to it. It's going to change the way business works."

Academics, I scoffed as I laughed at his wild fantasies.

I sold a load of Data General Ones to H. Ross Perot's company EDS. My briefcase technomiracles were high priced for individual consumers, so I thought volume sales with very little markup would be my secret. Hoping to make another big sale, I pitched John McDevitt, president of TSM Inc.—the holding company of Thomas S. Monaghan, the founder of Domino's Pizza and the only billionaire in Ann Arbor, Michigan. John told me to get lost and take my overpriced electric typewriters with me—but that would not be the last he saw of me.

I applied for a job at the future Domino's Farms Office Park. When they called me back, I thought, *Finally, this business economics degree is paying off!*

I learned later that they hired me because of a single line on my résumé: that I used to install sprinklers for my dad. I knew this to be essentially digging ditches. They thought I would be helpful on the organic farm Tom wanted, and they put me to work pricing organic vegetables on a produce wagon.

On week two someone asked if anyone knew anything about telephones.

"I do!" I said. (I mean, my brother is an engineer!) Then I spent several nights afterward at the library reading about phone systems. I discovered a mistake the electrical architects were making on a new building Tom wanted. I pointed out to them that they needed to be installing coaxial cable in the places where they were installing twisted pair. I turned out to be right and saved the day. Suddenly I was working sixteen-hour days doing my part to ensure Tom's building would be ready on time. I read all night and signed change orders all day, righting wrongs, averting disasters, and getting things done. I had no idea that every time I signed a change order, I was spending Tom's money. Without knowing it, I think I signed hundreds of thousands of Tom's dollars over to contractors. No wonder they liked me so much.

In the end, the building was ready on time, Tom was happy, and my sins were not only forgiven, but I had advanced from produce wagon to phone guy, to construction expediter, to property manager, to director of operations at Domino's Farms, the world headquarters of Domino's Pizza.

One day John McDevitt, the TSM Inc. president who sent me and my Data Generals packing, called me into his office.

"I want you to work for me," he said.

"I *do* work for you, John," I said. I was quite a few notches below him on the Domino's ladder.

"No, I want you to come up to the fourth floor and put your office right outside mine. Nothing gets to me except through you, and everything that goes out goes through you. You'll do all the talking to my administrative assistant. You'll be my gatekeeper. And I want you to start right now."

"Yes, sir," I said.

John held up three pages of single-spaced, handwritten notes on a pad.

"I get one of these every day from Tom Monaghan. I want you to go through this report every morning to help me focus on our priorities and ensure appropriate follow-through to exceed Tom's expectations."

Suddenly I was privy to political wars, money crunches, dealings with investment bankers, and all the high-stakes games multimillionaires play. I read John T. Molloy's *Dress for Success*, learned about investing in suits, the power of shirts, and the status of ties. I shined my shoes to look the part.

I was amazed by the environment of opportunity at Domino's Pizza. I got a broker's license, learned how to manage property, and learned about budgeting, forecasting, reporting, and people management. I started companies, learned how to frame and sell a project, how to convince others to get involved, and how to overcome any obstacle. If Tom said, "I want our office to be on Frank Lloyd Wright Drive," we figured out how to work with the city to name the street.

Frank Lloyd Wright was Tom's hero. All his life Wright had envisioned a decentralized, semi-urban development concept called Broadacre City where farm, factory, and family home exist side by side. Tom read a book called *How to Make $100,000 Farming 25 Acres*. Before long, its author, a regenerative farming pioneer and professor of Agriculture at Tuskegee University named Booker T. Whatley was in Ann Arbor helping us envision an organic farm. In part, the farm was intended to communicate freshness and health to pizza customers. In part it was Tom's homage to Frank Lloyd Wright's Broadacre City. Tom's visionary world was one in which anything that could be conceived could be achieved.

Mr. Monaghan's life's work extended beyond business to ministry. He established Catholic organizations that focused on education, media, ethics, and community projects. Later, he poured all of his time and fortune into these causes, but back in the late 1980s, Tom's world was an exciting one of wealth and celebrity. My office was across the hall from that of the French actor and mime artist Marcel Marceau. Some of the offices had stuffed wild animals and some had showers, which I had never before considered an office amenity. I had a small role in building Tom's multimillion-dollar two-story office with a silk ceiling, leather floor, mahogany walls, and a bathroom with a gold-flecked ceiling. I knew which brick I could lean on in an emergency to be rescued by private security agents. Tom was generous with his staff. He gave out big salaries and had mountain cabins for his executive teams. He let us play on his Drummond Island golf course and flew us there in his Gulfstream jet. He installed a helipad right outside his office window and flew to work in a Sikorsky S-76 helicopter. He had just bought the Detroit Tigers baseball team and would lend us the owner's box, where we ate steak sandwiches, watched games, and cracked open the window for a little crowd noise.

One year the Tigers swept the playoffs and won the World Series. Fans went wild in the streets of Detroit, overturning cars and setting them on fire. Hundreds of sports writers and stragglers were left stranded inside Tiger Stadium. Suddenly they heard the distinctive whir of rotors overhead, then watched Tom's Sikorsky S-76 land behind second base to deliver hundreds of Domino's pizzas to the stranded crowd.

If you befriended the right pilots and security agents, you might convince them to take you for a spin over the longest linear office structure on earth under the world's biggest copper roof. You would look down on the world's biggest collection of Frank Lloyd Wright artifacts and a classic car collection featuring Rolls-Royces from the 1920s and '30s, a Gullwing Mercedes, the Packard that took Franklin Delano Roosevelt to his second inauguration, and a handmade Bugatti Royale. You would look down on a distribution center, radio station, residences, warehouses, conference center, organic farm, petting zoo, and fields of Chianina cattle, American bison, giant Shire horses, and the tiny "Pizza Ponies" that marched in local parades.

Given his creativity, it came as no surprise when Tom said he wanted to build the world's longest nativity scene at the Domino's Christmas Light Show. It would be no easy task, in part because Tom was not universally loved. He is a devout Catholic and a pro-life advocate, which did not endear him to everyone in the liberal college town of Ann Arbor, Michigan. A coalition of neighbors opposed the light show and sued with a claim of nuisance. Then they hit us with a separate lawsuit saying a piece of Tom's property had been used to hold church services without appropriate zoning. It was easy for the press to paint Tom as a rich, conservative, corporate goliath against the little college town and miss another side to the story—beginning when 225,000 people showed up to our light show and dropped coins totaling $117,000 in our buckets for the benefit of several charities, including a windmill in Senegal.

Next thing I knew I was in Senegal, asking my host, Lộc Lê Châu, how he ended up out there in the desert.

"I was colonel in the South Vietnamese army fighting the French when I was shot," he said. "I was bleeding on the side of the road when my mom found me and hid me out in a monastery. My mom and those Catholic monks saved my life. I was a Buddhist. I didn't intend to convert to Catholicism. I just appreciated that they had saved my life—I was greatly loved by them, so I am compelled to love, and this is where I find myself."

That line—"I was greatly loved, so I am compelled to love"—got stuck in my head like a familiar song.

We went to a community where women and girls walked great distances each day to fetch water from an unprotected spring. They were forced to leave nursing babies at home. They were exposed to human and natural dangers along the way. Gastrointestinal disease was rampant, and people were dying from diseases that should have been eradicated ages ago.

We went to another community where a water project had been completed a few months earlier. People looked healthier, and they were planting little seedlings in plastic bags. They watered hundreds of seedlings on dozens of big trays in a makeshift nursery. They told us they were going to settle in this area, plant things, and grow roots. They were not just thinking about survival anymore. They were thinking about building homes and planning for the future.

We went to a community where they had completed a water project more than a year ago. People had permanent homes. Children laughed and ran around at a freshly painted school. They had surplus food, owned businesses, and had a sense of life together as a community.

It felt like I had traveled back in time one hundred years, then fifty, then to today, where I could see a vision of the future—and all the community needed to get here was *water*. Water gave them time. Time gave them the ability to grow food. Food gave them health, and they sold their surplus, which gave them cash resources, which gave them the ability to buy paint, pay school fees, and invest in children, business,

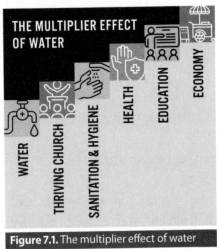

Figure 7.1. The multiplier effect of water

health, and home. I now know this is called the multiplier effect of water, but I was seeing it for the first time, and it blew my mind.

When Lộc Lê Châu stood on that rock and preached a sermon on the water of life in French, the national language of Senegal, its simultaneous translation into Wolof and English conjured images of Pentecost for me, each of us hearing good news in our native tongue. And just like the Pentecost crowd, we were filled with the Holy Spirit, singing, dancing, laughing, and shouting. Onlookers watching crusty old Max lead a line of dancing Muslim children shouting, "Alleluia!" and "Praise Jesus!" may have thought we'd had too much wine. Everyone was focused, not on our differences, but on the love, joy, and appreciation for life and health we all held in common.

I marveled at what a miracle it was that we accessed water hundreds of meters below us. It was a miracle that God somehow wove together stories of lawsuits against a Catholic pizza mogul in Michigan, giggling Muslim Wolof kids, a chain-smoking windmill prophet, a Christian charity, and a community of once-nomadic goat herders into one story of one Body in Christ being tickled by the Holy Spirit. It was a miracle that even I—Mike, the ditch-digger from Escalon—was part of this story. Since that was the case, I wanted to find some way to work, not for an Ann Arbor business genius, but for God, the Master Strategist.

I am greatly loved, so I am compelled to love—the words still rang in my head, but where would I find myself? I was not Lộc Lê Châu. I had never commanded troops. I could not speak French. I could not survive in this desert. I was just a twenty-seven-year-old aspiring businessman who'd bought new camping pants with zip-off legs for an African adventure.

Back home, I repeated Lộc Lê Châu's words as a daily prayer—*I am greatly loved, so I am compelled to love. Please open a door!* I wanted to work for God, but nothing happened. I'd had a taste of participating in God's work, and I wanted more. I served on the board of a little Christian school and volunteered in a soup kitchen, but it all felt so small. I longed to be part of something *big* like what I had witnessed in Senegal. For three years straight I prayed that prayer every day, longing to do great things for the Master Strategist, but only little things came my way. I understood God to be telling me he did not need me to do great things, but rather to be faithful in little things and observe those who came before me doing great things.

One of these was my father-in-law, Reverend Juan Boonstra. Few of us know what our parents really do for a living, and even fewer of us understand the work of our spouse's parents. "The Rev" and I had not yet warmed up to each other relationally when he invited me to join him on a trip to Guatemala. I knew he traveled a lot to his home country of Argentina and throughout Latin America, so I jumped at the chance to accompany him to Guatemala City. I thought he would be preaching at some small church and perhaps I could slip away for an adventure. He had some important meetings to attend, so I made it easy on both of us and let him know that I would dust off my rusty Spanish and take a look around for a couple of days.

I heard the call of a "Chicken Bus" driver, "Sola, Sola, Sololá!" and took it to the end of the line, near Lake Atitlan, at which point I climbed into a tiny van, overloaded with farmers and families, all dressed in beautifully woven, well-worn clothing. I hitched rides around the lake on a tractor and in the back of pickup trucks to discover that each village had its own beautiful pattern of clothing that historically identified its wearers to keep them from escaping slave labor. I was negotiating to purchase a pair of shorts with intricately stitched birds when I heard my father-in-law's voice coming from a radio inside the vendor's home.

"I know that man!" I said.

My almost involuntary exclamation led to a shared Coca Cola with the vendor and a talk about Juan's radio program *La Hora de la Reforma*, the good news of Jesus Christ, and the church life around the lake.

When I returned to Guatemala City a couple of days later, I was taken aback by my ordinarily formal father-in-law's warm embrace as we exchanged stories. I discovered that I had naively been wandering through a dangerous area deeply involved in the country's civil war. I was also surprised to learn that instead of preaching in little Guatemalan churches, he had been meeting with church and university leaders and heads of state to discuss national and continental ministry issues. As I thought about it later, I think he hugged me for this first time because he was relieved not to have to return to his beloved daughter in the United States bearing bad news of a lost son-in-law. Following this escapade, we became best friends, and I learned that ministry can be very complex and sophisticated.

I kept working for Tom Monaghan and kept gaining more responsibility. Then one day an executive from World Vision, one of the world's largest Christian relief and development organizations, whom I had met through the Christmas light show, asked me to apply for a fundraising position in Grand Rapids, Michigan.

The offer did not fit my idea of doing big things for God. By this time, I thought of myself as a hard-soled blue-suit kind of guy. I thought a soft-soled nonprofit fundraising job was beneath me, but Natalie thought I should consider it. Believing that I was lowering myself to the task, I applied for the job—and they hired someone else! They rejected me! It felt like my first week at Word of God when a chaste, impoverished, floor-sleeping monk was telling me what to do, except this time I was not even good enough to join.

I kept praying that prayer, and a year later World Vision approached me with a new idea. They said they wanted to invest in America's inner cities while simultaneously raising money for water, food, education, and microcredit programs around the world. They told me Borg-Warner CEO Jim Bere was behind this vision, and so was the Chicago urban ministry pioneer, Bill Leslie. They just needed someone like me, a hard-soled blue-suit kind of guy who could fly around the world but who also knew his way around media, politicians, businesspeople, and church groups in major US cities. "You," they said, "are the new breed of field rep." Their proposal appealed to my inflated sense of self. It was tempting, but I thought I should just stay in my lane as a businessman.

Natalie disagreed.

"Either stop praying God will open a door," she said, "or when God does open a door, walk through it."

She was right, so I told John McDevitt I planned to commit three years to God's service as a tithe on my professional life. He quizzed me as to why.

After explaining my thought process to my tough yet deeply spiritual boss and mentor, John responded, "You didn't mention money?" I told him that this one was not about the money. He nodded and then reassured me that he'd help me investigate the opportunity and if the organization checked out and I still believed God was behind the invitation, he would back me 100 percent.

Then he added, "How do we replace you?"

"I've got you covered," I said. "Same make, different model, different year. Hire my brother Pete. He'll be your man for three years, and when I return, I'll take back my job."

With that, Pete went to work at Domino's Farms. Finally, I had paid him back for gathering enough beer bottle money to rent my crutches.

As I arranged all this, I assumed that if I followed God's will, God would take care of me. What I did not know was that God's vision and timing may not be the same as my own. Natalie, our two daughters, Libby and Abbi, and I moved to Chicago and rented a high-rise apartment on Lake Shore Drive. Meanwhile, our house did not sell, so we were paying our mortgage in addition to expensive downtown rent. We had not yet learned to live on less money, and we were spending more than we were earning. Then a bizarre series of events unfolded:

Jim Bere, the president of the auto parts manufacturing giant whose money was behind the vision of the "new breed" I was supposed to represent, had a fatal heart attack.

Bill Leslie, the creative urban ministry pioneer who backed the same vision, also had a heart attack and died.

The head of US programs at World Vision who had promoted the vision internally experienced a serious stroke.

The guy who was going to be my direct supervisor resigned, and so did his supervisor who had interviewed me. When I looked around, I saw that *everyone* behind the vision of me as the "new breed of field rep" was gone. A year later, I had still not secured a single significant gift for World Vision, and my job was on the line.

While I was struggling to sort out how to move forward without any of the original visionaries, one of my colleagues told me about a similar situation World Vision had encountered in Romania when working with medical and university systems there to address the orphanage crisis after the fall of the Ceausescu regime in 1989. They had engaged thought leaders from Case Western Reserve University (CWRU) who pitched to World Vision this crazy idea that transformation does not come from talking about what is broken and what you want to fix, but rather from talking about what works and where you want to go. He told me the approach enabled World Vision to rebuild hospitals and university infrastructure in Romania, and that it could do the same in America's inner cities.

Under the guidance of a pair of pioneers in organizational behavior from CWRU, David Cooperrider[1] and Jim Ludema,[2] we started
systematically investigating what was *right* with the church in
Chicago through an initiative we called Vision Chicago. Jim led us
through a series of appreciative inquiries that would positively
change how churches engage with each other in the city and open
my eyes to how nonprofit organizations could empower the church
to transform the world. By reaching out to what I thought were
remote stakeholders, we quickly discovered that our cities are
brimming with outstanding leaders who are sorely underresourced.
I met men and women who were feeding the poor and running
daycare centers, homeless shelters, and leadership development
programs where our nation needs them most. Each of the churches
I visited appeared to be an oasis in a desert. In many of our lowest-
income and most dangerous neighborhoods, the local church was a
very visible, positive contributor to public life.

I learned about the powerful Reverend Dr. Lincoln Scott in
Lawndale, the West Side Chicago neighborhood that was home to
gangs like the Vice Lords and Satan's Disciples. I camped out in his
antechamber a few hours a week for nearly a month, hoping to meet
him. When he finally saw me, I explained that I was new with World
Vision, I worked in church collaborations, and I was trying to raise
money for worthy inner-city programs.

"I don't need your money," said Dr. Scott.

Shocked and embarrassed, I asked, "Well, then, what do you need?"

"I need to be able to show people what God is doing here, but
everyone's afraid to set foot in this neighborhood—I need exposure."

Still desperate to secure a donation and keep my job, I started calling
my contacts in the wealthy North Shore neighborhood and eventually
introduced myself to a woman named Amy in her North Shore bookstore.

"I no longer support World Vision," she said. "We have so many
needs in our own city. I don't send money overseas anymore."

"That's perfect," I said. "I'm organizing a mission trip to the inner city right here in Chicago, and you should go. I'd like you to invite your pastor too."

She agreed, and now I had two recruits for my trip. Within a week, we were driving a busload of senior pastors and their members to Lincoln Scott's church and homeless shelter in Lawndale. We had a long meal of smothered pork chops, cornbread, and collard greens at a local soul food restaurant and listened as everyone told their story.

Dr. Lincoln Scott related how one cold night in the late 1980s, he had passed two homeless men as he walked home from his church. The men were drinking and shooting up in an abandoned building, not an unusual sight in Lawndale. The next day the two men's bodies lay dead outside Reverend Dr. Scott's church. They had died of hypothermia. The tragedy inspired Dr. Scott to open Hope House, a food pantry and residential homeless shelter that ministered to recovering addicts and people transitioning back into society after incarceration.

As we said goodbye, we all held hands and prayed in the parking lot of Lincoln Scott's Church of God in Christ. Sister Scott, the first lady of that church, prayed through tears for God to save Hope House from the City of Chicago, which threatened to close it down.

Days later I got a call from our community organizer who told me that the city indeed intended to take Hope House away. Though the shelter was tax exempt, he explained, Dr. Scott had been renting a corner of the building to a local grocer and had not paid taxes on that portion of his building. The cost to save the building was $35,000. I called Amy, explained the situation, and asked if I could call her pastor.

"He doesn't have any money," she said, "He's a pastor!"

Desperately, I pleaded, "Well, who has money?"

"I have some money," she said, "and actually, I've been praying since our visit. I think God told me to give Dr. Scott $10,000 . . . but I need to expand my bookstore, so I'm going to give $5,000."

I called Dr. Scott and shared the good news.

"You call her right back," he said, "and you tell her that if God told her to give $10,000, she has to give $10,000!"

"Amy," I sheepishly reported to her, "Pastor Scott said you have to give the whole $10k if that's what God told you to do."

"Who do I make out the check to?" she asked. "World Vision or Hope House?"

I paused for a while, wanting badly for that check to go to World Vision so I could keep my job, which was just starting to get interesting.

"Make it out to Hope House," I said reluctantly, and that very night Amy met me halfway in the Loyola University parking lot.

"Mike," she said as she handed me the check, "don't you let that shelter close!"

Even though it was late at night, I drove straight to Lawndale, and handed the check to Dr. Scott with a great sense of purpose.

Months later, Dr. Scott told me about a dream in which he had died. He saw bright lights pass by him as he moved from our earthly realm toward God. He said he felt a great sense of shame that he had not finished his work on earth. He felt especially deep shame that at the hour of his death the city was poised to confiscate his shelter. Feeling the weight of all he had left to do, he begged God not to take him home.

"God turned me around," Dr. Scott told me, "and as he sent me back God said, 'Those lights you see, those are angels I'm sending you,' and you, Mike Mantel, *you* are one of those angels. You brought that $10,000 from Amy. Another fella you brought here gave us $25,000. Those two gifts saved Hope House, then you helped us to write that grant for $1.5 million. I never left my property, and God just kept sending me angels, and you were one of them."

Stories like that repeated over and over again. It was exhilarating. I became like an addict, wanting again and again to identify what God was doing and to join that activity. Over and over, impossible things were made possible as we tried to collectively discern God's will and join that work. All the skills I learned working for Tom's companies—

budgeting, forecasting, reporting, people management, and how to frame and sell a project, convince others to get involved, and overcome obstacles—I now applied all those skills to God's work. We kept hosting urban mission trips inviting pastors from the suburbs to no longer pass over the inner-city neighborhoods but to identify and cross the lines that divide us. We asked them to join hands with their neighbors, listening to their concerns, praying together, and working together to improve our city and the world.

A number of churches started to define their mission field in terms of "Jerusalem," "Judea and Samaria," and "the ends of the earth" (see Acts 1:8). They had come to understand *Jerusalem* as their neighborhood; *Judea and Samaria*, the rest of Chicago; and *the ends of the earth*, a community in some other country with whom they chose to link arms. At first some churches assumed that a global nonprofit would dilute their local focus or cut into their collection plate. The opposite turned out to be the case. Working together across geographical boundaries increased our shared understanding, expanded resources, and made us more effective at the level of the local church, the city, and the world.

Most Christians know God wants our faith to have a wide impact, yet few churches are equipped for the linguistic, cultural, and logistical challenges of city-wide and global ministry. For both wealthy and low-income suburban churches and wealthy and low-income urban ones, our partnership made it easier and less expensive to reach out across the world. People got excited about having a global impact and gave more, not less, to their local church, because it was enriching to know their impact would extend "to the ends of the earth."

On a city-wide level, churches generally want to improve their city, but they don't know where to start. They often lack familiarity with municipal-level processes, politicians, corporate leaders, and urban ministry networks that can help. It became our job to make these connections, get people together, pray, and follow the Lord's leading.

What began as Vision Chicago was later adopted as "Vision Cities" by World Vision and its partners in New York, Los Angeles, and other domestic US cities. On a global level, it was immensely exciting for churches across Chicago to team up, for example, to build a hospital at the heart of the HIV/AIDS crisis in Zambia. Churches in Zambia were excited to be empowered to minister to the sick. Understanding the HIV/AIDS crisis on a global level also helped churches here and there overcome prejudice against people suffering from AIDS and participate in Jesus' healing work.

Many churches that had lacked the ability to effectively engage their highest capacity changemakers experienced a benefit by joining forces with us. One businessman, Chuck Brewer, wanted badly to make a big difference in God's kingdom, but he was frustrated. His pastors suggested he become an usher or volunteer to paint a church in Nicaragua, but he felt his skills could contribute to something bigger. Aiming for big impact, he showed up at a Sunday food drive with a semi-trailer filled with provisions. It had seemed like a good idea, but his effort ended up demoralizing all the families that showed up with bags of canned goods in the trunks of their Ford Fiestas.

Working with this businessman, his pastors, and ministry visionary Gordon Murphy, we gathered a group of high-level executives and named ourselves the Wiseguys. Murphy was a gifted bridge builder and friend maker. He understood loyalty and how to create enough structure—blended with honesty, humor, and shared mission—so that people would be willing to risk engagement across the lines that divide us. He taught us to do the same. We dreamed of investing our business principles and skills to serve the Lord and help at-risk communities rebuild. We harnessed our collective knowledge, skills, political connections, and corporate relationships to develop The Storehouse, a big-box building-material warehouse for low-income people. The idea was to ask manufacturers and suppliers to donate their surplus or out-of-date products for a tax break and offer these products to inner-city churches who were rebuilding their places of worship and helping their congregants improve their homes. The handling fees paid the operational costs of The Storehouse. Everybody won as the church became more visible and relevant with vital home improvement projects while simultaneously enabling us to be missionaries in the boardrooms of major American corporations.

Figure 7.2. The Storehouse brought church and business together to serve the community

Everyone's lives were changed in the process—churches and individuals alike, rich and poor, urban and suburban, in our city and across the world. We represented one united global body of Christ.

In Chicago, I learned that Christians can cross deeply entrenched dividing lines not only to further their own goals but to stretch into a bigger vision. As we overcame division, the Holy Spirit was able to use us beyond our own imaginations, and we found that we were also blessed beyond our imaginations. Our diversity gave us a powerful view, both of our city and the world. I found that with what we learn in our cities, we can contribute more globally; and the more we learn globally, the better we can contribute within our cities.

The whole story of Scripture culminates with a vision of a Holy City, the new Jerusalem (Revelation 21:2). The image mirrors the Garden of Eden. Our story began in the perfect world God gave us, and the biblical vision is for our story to end in the perfect city God will create with our participation—the product of our collective efforts, "a new heaven and a new earth," together as one at last (Revelation 21:1). This is the vision of the redeemed world into which God calls us—and it may as well begin with the world within *your* city.

Reflect

Jew or Gentile, slave or free, male or female—these were the divisions Paul mentioned in his letter to the church in Galatia. What are the lines that divide us today?

Write

Consider the various dividing lines in your city or community that you or your church community could cross in order to look more like Christ.

Share

Talk to someone you trust about which dividing line you'd like to cross in your city. Then take one specific action to build a bridge.

TOGETHER WE CAN TRANSFORM THE WORLD

As you sent me into the world,
I have sent them into the world.

JOHN 17:18

HAVING GIVEN ME a taste of the power of unity in action, I was ready for God to expand my boundaries to the wider world.

The stories of this reflection illustrate that our collective voice becomes a fuller likeness of God's as we connect across the lines that divide us into denominations, genders, ethnicities, and political parties. Working together, we are equipped for a bigger vision, a deeper strategy, and a better product.

These stories also illustrate that including diverse voices is not always easy, and it does not always result in immediate harmony. To the contrary, including diverse perspectives can expose important conflicts and injustices that may have otherwise remained buried. Scripture offers no guarantees that participating in God's work will be easy, but it does offer a vision of a partnership with God that will transform the world.

As you read this story, I invite you to consider when and how you have joined forces with people who are different from you to accomplish something better together than you could have done alone.

IIIIIIIIIIIIIIIIIIIIIIIII

When I began working there, World Vision's fundraising office was at 122 South Michigan Avenue, across from the Art Institute of Chicago. If you don't know Chicago, that's a block from Cloud Gate, the shiny silver bean sculpture always featured in shots of The Windy City. Our offices were on the twenty-second floor of the Peoples Gas Building. In 1911, architect Daniel Burnham covered the entrance of that building with marble from the quarry from which the marble for the Parthenon was mined. This was, and always had been, the place to be if you want to hang out with rich people, which was my job as a fundraiser.

As a result of shared strategy planning, we opened a program office at 5001 West Harrison on Chicago's infamous West Side, known to some for crime, drugs, and violent gangs. The city had agreed to give us a run-down, former–Chicago Public Schools book distribution center if we could use it to benefit our city. This was the warehouse that the Wiseguys converted into The Storehouse.

My friend, academic mentor, and fellow Christian Jim Ludema had moved from Case Western Reserve University to Benedictine University just outside of Chicago. He taught me how to leverage the church's strengths to transform our city and to incorporate a broad range of voices into our strategy, including those of the people with whom we serve—and those people did not usually hang out at 122 South Michigan Ave across from the Art Institute.

After the experience with Dr. Scott and Amy, I decided that we should move our fundraising office into The Storehouse. Now we had marketers, fundraisers, community organizers, Wiseguys, customer service people, and pastors interacting under one roof daily. We formed a leadership team that put an African American pastor, the Reverend George Wilson, in charge of our church engagement strategy; a Puerto Rican named Ivan Gonzalez in charge of operations for The Storehouse; and a White woman, Amber Johnson, leading the marketing team. We were Black, Hispanic, and White. Our core management team was Pentecostal, Presbyterian, Lutheran, Baptist, and Catholic—all of us with different styles of prayer and worship—and our diversity made us stronger. We used to joke that we needed Pentecostals on our team to hear God's voice and Presbyterians to operationalize what he told us to do.

With our diverse leadership team in place, I was eager to engage their experience, intelligence, and prayer in the next big thing God would have for us, so we turned to Appreciative Inquiry, the strengths-based strategic planning approach I had learned from David Cooperrider and Jim Ludema. Appreciative Inquiry was developed as a *social* process for including voices from all the stakeholders in a system to articulate their best practices and shared vision, but I was curious to see how the process would fare as a social *and* spiritual discernment process among Christians. These participants would look to prayer and discerning God's will through the communion of saints; they would ask God questions and invite God to interact with them. I was excited about Appreciative Inquiry as a tool for strategic planning, also, to help us take risks and move into the unknown with the confidence that God led the way.

I was captivated by the notion inherent in Appreciative Inquiry that language is not just descriptive but generative. In Genesis, God speaks the world into being with words: "Let there be light" (Genesis 1:3). The theme of God's creative word pops up throughout the Bible: "By the word of the Lord the heavens were made," writes the psalmist; "By faith we understand that the universe was created by the word of God," writes the author of Hebrews; and "the Word became flesh," John writes in his gospel (Psalm 33:6; Hebrews 11:3 ESV; John 1:14). I was learning that through prayerful dialogue with God and his people, we can discern his will. I was fascinated by the idea that God creates through the word, and as image-bearers, we also create through our words. As our new team developed a two-day strategic planning summit, we bathed the process in prayer. I could not wait to see how we would collect, form, and validate our words to co-create with God.

I was reminded of my daughters' pleas, "Swing me again!" Now, I was once again shouting to God, only this time with a whole team shouting, "Swing *us* again!"

I went into the prayer and planning summit pretty sure God would call us more deeply into water ministry. I had known that was my destiny ever since the day God spoke to me in Senegal. I was not wrong about that destiny, but I was about to find out that my idea of *when* it would happen was not aligned with God's.

To my utter dismay, participants at our summit started talking about being called to help people suffering from a disease called HIV/AIDS. I thought it was a terrible idea. To begin with, I knew nothing at all about it. It was mysterious and controversial, especially among Christians who at the time associated it with promiscuity, illegal drugs, and homosexuality. It would be a hard sell among our supporters. Christians didn't even like to talk about sex, much less sexually transmitted infections (STIs), this one least of all. Why chain ourselves to something so unpopular? There were so many other causes that people actually wanted to support.

Water, for example, was simple and clear. Nothing makes a greater impact. Water is the basis of all life. Access to safe drinking water eases the burden on women. It helps people grow food. It saves the lives of children and babies—and what Christian doesn't love babies?

Fortunately, I thought, I know how the Appreciative Inquiry process works, and I started inserting the idea of water into conversations here and there, planting seeds wherever I could. Yet try as I might, the current of the conversation kept flowing toward this deadly STD. This came completely out of the blue for me. I was not aware of anyone in our staff or constituency being interested in HIV/AIDS, yet the topic seemed to hold them like a spell. It was fundraising suicide, and by the end of day one I was losing hope that I would talk them off the ledge.

As day two began, I hoped they had returned to their senses after a good night's sleep. But no such luck. They were still talking about HIV and AIDS. I continued offering my stump speeches about water where I could, to no avail. I could not believe it.

There is a moment on day two of an Appreciative Inquiry Summit when all the participants stand before a huge mind map on the wall. At its center is the organization's "positive core of strengths" and "compelling vision of the future." Out from that core emanate all the different things the group has envisioned for its future. To determine which will receive energy, time, and attention, each participant gets five stickers to stick to the mind map by the programs and activities they want to prioritize. My heart sank as I watched stickers pile up on HIV/AIDS activities, leaving all my water program ideas high and dry.

Next, there is a "fishbowl discussion." Leaders sit in the middle of the room surrounded by participants as they discuss. I was drowned in that fishbowl by the voices of my colleagues. There was simply nothing I could say to get HIV off the table or get H_2O on it.

For those too young to remember the HIV/AIDS crisis at its height, please let me offer some context. Our ministry primarily worked with the church, and many Christians wanted nothing to do with the disease. A 2001 poll conducted by the Barna Research Group revealed that only 3 percent of evangelical Christians said they would be willing to help an AIDS orphan in Africa.[1] My colleagues in Chicago felt that it was the leprosy of our day, ours to heal, just as Jesus healed lepers. Other Christians disagreed.

Another reason the disease elicited such strong opinions is that we fear what we do not understand. For many of the years AIDS was killing people, it was a medical mystery. Nobody even knew what it was. I knew nothing about it myself, even years after it was identified by scientists. To illustrate how confusing the AIDS pandemic was, let's compare it to a more recent one.

Covid-19 came to the attention of the World Health Organization (WHO) as a new "viral pneumonia" on December 31, 2019. Two weeks later the Chinese government reported that it had not only identified the novel coronavirus but also mapped its genetic sequence and shared it with the world.[2] The first known case was later traced back to November. According to information available at the time of this writing, only two months passed between the day the disease first infected a human and the day its viral cause was mapped.[3] Whatever the actual timeline turns out to be, the virus remained a mystery for weeks or months, but not years.

HIV, by contrast, evaded identification for decades. Even after AIDS was being carefully studied by scientists around the world, it took years to identify its viral cause. And it was not until 1986 that a consensus was reached about what the virus should be called: HIV, for Human Immunodeficiency Virus.[4]

Those years of confusion produced countless myths and rumors about HIV and AIDS. People said you could get it from toilet seats in public restrooms. Could you get it from kissing? What about an infected food handler at a restaurant? Would the virus become airborne and kill us all? Would there ever be a cure? Or treatment? Nobody knew. All these uncertainties in science and society clouded my enthusiasm for investing the team's effort into this cause.

An Appreciative Inquiry Summit consists of four stages: Discovery, Dream, Design, and Delivery. First, you *discover* the collection of assets and what already works well in the organization. Next, you *dream* of the desired future state. For us, this involved prayerful discernment. Then you *design*, meaning plan and prioritize processes to achieve your vision. Then *delivery* refers to the execution of that design.

In our design phase, the team determined that step one of our strategy would be to launch an HIV/AIDS response through the Black church in Chicago. Step two would be to expand our vision to all churches across Chicago and the Midwest, but only after Black churches had blazed the trail. Step three would be to involve businesses and other institutions, but only after the church had made its stand.

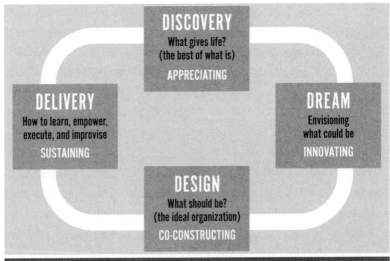

Figure 8.1. The Appreciative Inquiry Summit process

It was an unconventional strategy. In every successful program I had ever seen, we first got big money involved, then big churches, with smaller churches joining in later. Not only did the team want to drag me into a thorny pandemic, but they wanted to do it with a backward fundraising strategy. Even more challenging, we would start our work across the world, in Africa.

Exhausted as the summit drew to a close, I went to my office to be alone and think. The Reverend George Wilson was there waiting for me.

"Mike," Pastor Wilson said, "I want to talk to you." He was a powerful man with strong opinions who always let them be known.

"What's up, Pastor?" I asked with a smile.

"I understand that World Vision is going to have a forum in New York on the topic of HIV and AIDS."

World Vision had gathered a lineup of speakers for an event to which fundraisers like me could invite wealthy donors and prospects, first to learn about the challenges of the church and the world including HIV/AIDS, and second to respond financially.

"We need to invite some significant Black pastors to that forum," Pastor Wilson pressed, "to implement the strategy God led us to with the opportunities God puts in front of us."

He had a point. I remembered praying for years for an open door to serve God, and Natalie telling me to stop praying for an open door if I wasn't going to go through it. Either I believed God had guided our process or I didn't. George started reciting his invitation list. He wanted to invite Bishop Horace E. Smith, MD, a pediatric hematologist who led the Apostolic Faith Church. He wanted to invite the head of COGIC, the Church of God in Christ, America's biggest Pentecostal denomination. He had a young and fiery activist preacher on his list, and another West Side pastor and political influencer. It was an impressive list of influential denominational leaders, pastors of large churches, and leaders of city-wide movements and networks. Seeing the relevance of his plan, I told him I would back him 100 percent.

Then George took a moment to explain to me how hospitality and invitation work in his culture. He said we would not only need to pay for them, but as a matter of respect we would need to host them appropriately. What he described was a far cry from the covered-dish potluck hospitality of my Dutch Christian Reformed Church upbringing, but I took his word for it. I found a couple of donors who bought into the vision we'd crafted and covered their costs to attend The Forum.

The first night of The Forum ended with the powerful testimony of Princess Kasune Zulu from Zambia. She held us spellbound as she described losing her baby sister to a mystery disease when she was a child, then her mother, then her father, leaving her responsible for her grandparents and siblings.

In search of stability, she married an older Zambian man, Moffat Zulu. Later, she was volunteering at a hospital through her church when she found herself drawn to patients who had the same symptoms as the disease that killed her parents. She learned that they had a disease called AIDS, which came from a virus called HIV. It occurred to her that two of her husband's three previous wives had died of a mystery disease just like her parents.

When Princess went to be tested for HIV, she was shocked as the doctor told her that under Zambian law, she needed her husband's permission to be tested. Moffat did not want to know if either of them had HIV because of the stigma and immense social and economic pressure resulting from a positive diagnosis. After four months of Princess asking, he finally granted permission. They both tested HIV-positive.

Astounded that nobody in Zambia was talking about this mystery disease, Princess started a school for AIDS orphans. It was rewarding, but she knew that no support could ever replace two living parents. She had to find a way to prevent the infection in the first place.

One day while her husband was at work, Princess put on a pair of tight jeans, high heels, red lipstick, and a short silk tank top. Disguised as a commercial sex worker, she started hitchhiking among truckers on the tradeways of Zambia to teach them about the dangers of HIV/AIDS. Then she started convincing companies to let her teach HIV/AIDS seminars to their employees. She was invited to talk about HIV and AIDS on a Catholic radio program. Audience call-ins were so high the station gave her a show of her own. Then she got a TV show.

Now she had been brought to New York City, out of Zambia for the first time, concluding her talk to World Vision's most prominent donors with a call-to-action aimed directly at the church:

Now the church in Africa and around the world needs to awaken!

If the church doesn't have compassion for those living with HIV and AIDS, who will?

If one brother, one sister, is sick regardless of where they are or who they are, we are all affected in one way or another.

The room was electric. We all erupted in a standing ovation, except for Bishop Smith, MD, who seemed preoccupied as he leaned across the table.

"Mike, is this young lady on meds?"

I had no idea what that meant.

"I don't know, Doctor," I responded. "Let me see what I can find out."

"Princess," I asked her after I tracked her down, "are you on meds?"

"Oh, unfortunately," she said, "we don't have the resources for antiretroviral drugs. They are far too expensive for us, so no, I'm not."

I reported back to Dr. Smith, still unaware of what antiretroviral meds were or what it meant to not be on them. But as I watched the Bishop's passions rise, I could tell I was about to find out.

"What do you mean she's not on antiretroviral medications?" the Bishop demanded.

During her talk, Princess mentioned that her CD4 count had dipped down to ninety-two at the time. It meant nothing to me, but to a hematologist like Bishop Smith it apparently meant a lot. The next forty-eight hours were a marathon of intense conversations about racial and institutional injustice. It was forty-eight hours of passion, anger, interrogation, and exasperation, deep into the night in hotel lobbies. It was intense, life changing, and quite different from the fancy fundraising dinner I set out to attend.

Throughout those forty-eight hours I continued to reach out to Princess to extend hospitality to her as a guest in our country. I asked her what she planned to do next, and she said she didn't know. She had a ticket home eventually but planned to spend some time in the United States, maybe to visit an African American acquaintance she had once met in Namibia. The acquaintance could not be reached, and she had no idea what she would do after that.

Over the course of those tense forty-eight hours, our group from Chicago decided that we would invite Princess and Moffat to Chicago, where Dr. Smith would lead the churches in taking care of the couple's health issues and where I would be in charge of their hospitality.

Antiretroviral, or ARV, medications cost a couple thousand dollars per month at the time. Moreover, those with HIV who begin ARV therapy have to stay on it for life. It was a significant ask to commit to this couple we had just met.

On the flight back to Chicago I was reading books about HIV and AIDS as fast as I could. I had four little girls at home, and I had no idea back then if it was safe to invite an HIV-positive couple into our home.

As soon as I got home, I convened a family meeting with Natalie and our four young girls: Libby, Abbi, Maggie, and Katie. I told them about meeting Princess and Moffat. Then I told them everything I knew about HIV and AIDS, which was a shotgun blast of not very much. I told them it was a virus, it was transmitted through blood and through body fluids, maybe saliva or maybe not. I told them I didn't know anything about food, or how we should be in proximity to people who had it. I told them this virus was killing people all over the world, and that women in Africa were dying even though they had nothing to do with their husbands' indiscretions while truck driving. I told them children were orphaned and dying, and that HIV/AIDS was a critical global crisis that was about to explode.

I explained to the girls that their mother and I were struggling with a dilemma: God requires that we be hospitable, especially to those in need, but I also believed it was my first responsibility to keep our children safe from the dangers of the world. Could we responsibly invite Princess and Moffat to stay in our home with all the unknown risks?

"Dad," eight-year-old Maggie replied, "we have no choice."

"Okay," I said, "but what is the 'no choice'?" Whatever was so clear to her was still very murky to me.

"Dad," Maggie said, "we *have* to invite Princess into our home. If God asks us to do it, and we obey, he'll protect us."

If you have faith like one of these little ones, I thought. Maggie's childlike faith suddenly brought clarity in the fog of my adult fears.

Princess and Moffat were delighted by the invitation. We had a pond behind our home where they caught a fish and prepared it for us to eat. I anxiously watched Princess gut it, knife in hand, afraid she would nick herself, bleed onto our food, and kill my children. I was a beginner at childlike faith, that's for sure.

Princess was also delighted by the prospect of living a longer life and sharing her story with Chicago churches. Dr. Smith invited his vast medical establishment to begin to address the complexity of Princess's health and an extended network of Black churches began to explore taking action to fight this terrible virus. Princess stayed in the Chicago area for a while before returning to Zambia. While she was in Chicago, the Wiseguys at The Storehouse got to know her. Later, one of them, a businessman named Jim Reid, said his wife, Tedde, had always wanted to go to Africa, so we gathered a group of medical professionals and Wiseguys and flew to Zambia. We landed in the capital, Lusaka, then took a short flight north to Kitwe, where Princess met up with us to show us around.

The group laughs when I remind them of the huge quantity of luggage we brought on that trip. The little commuter plane could not handle the weight of the luggage, so we hired a driver to transport it overland in a jeep as we flew overhead. In the years that followed, Jim and Tedde returned to Zambia fifteen times. After a couple of trips, we each learned to fit our travel gear into one twenty-six-pound carry-on. For me, this illustrated the profound truth that as individuals, families, churches, and nations, we hold tight to our possessions when we move into the unfamiliar.

The Reids and I started taking a new group to Zambia each year, to World Vision's ZamTan Area Development Program, which included an enormous slum outside the city of Kitwe formed when the Zambia-Tanzania Trucking Company went bankrupt, leaving its staff nowhere to go. Unable to pay rent, they built a shanty town with no water, no sewage, and no electricity.

One year we were excited about a new drug called Nevirapine, which prevented mother-to-baby HIV transmission during birth. It only cost

$1 for each pill—a buck a life!—yet Zambians were not using it. When we spoke to Zambian medical professionals, World Vision staff, church leaders, and community organizers, we were shocked to hear that none of them thought Zambian women would take the drug.

First, they said, most Zambian women do not give birth in hospitals, so administration would be a challenge. Women there give birth in homes. Even more heartbreakingly, they did not think women would take Nevirapine because knowing they themselves were going to die, they considered it cruel to leave babies alone in the world without a mother to care for them.

We had to figure out how to get ARV drugs to these mothers. World Vision had programmatically avoided ARV therapy up to now because of the $1,500-per-month price tag and the fact that it must be administered for life. Now we faced the same choice we did with Princess: Help just one woman at an astronomical price, or do nothing? We started looking for people who would commit to kicking in money each month for life. Inspired by the dedication of the Zambian medical professionals and health workers, the Wiseguys decided they needed to build a hospital.

"What do you need for a hospital?" Chuck Brewer asked in his gruff Chicago accent, throwing a manila envelope on the table at the Sherbourne Hotel in Kitwe. A World Vision Zambia health care worker drew a hospital on the envelope. She drew an infectious disease unit, maternity care, x-ray, laboratory, and everything she felt a rural Zambian hospital needed to respond to HIV/AIDS. Back in Chicago, Chuck handed that manila envelope over to his CAD/CAM guy, whose software turned it into professional building prints. Step-by-step, God guided us through what was needed to make the vision a reality. Led by Jim and Tedde Reid, we raised $1.2 million. We negotiated with the government to get doctors, which also involved building houses for the medical staff on the site. We were told that it would be impossible to assemble and install a fully functioning lab. Remarkably, my dad heard about a small organization that did just that at a "moment on mission" at the Ann Arbor Christian Reformed Church. Every step of the way we had the confidence to overcome obstacles because we knew God was leading the way.

When I visited ZamTan with the Reids about five years ago, that former slum had running water, electricity, and streets lined with stores and filled with clean and healthy families. They had medical facilities and schools. People were even moving there to retire. I think we met at least five children named Tedde there. We were not responsible for all that transformation, but we played our part, and as a result countless lives have been saved, thousands have been treated in that hospital, and we all received the incomparable experience of finding our role in God's plan for us and for the world.

Figure 8.2. The World Vision Zambia–envisioned local hospital becomes a reality

As the Father sent Jesus into the world, Jesus sent Princess into the world, and she transformed our lives and many others. After her time with us, Princess went on to charm one audience after another, including one at the White House where President George W. Bush asked her to share her story. After that meeting, the President kissed Princess on the cheek as camera strobes flashed. A photo of the kiss appeared in USA Today the next day, then later in the media in the UK, Australia, Kenya, Nigeria, South Africa, Botswana, Singapore, and other countries. A photo of the President of the United States kissing an HIV-positive African woman sent a powerful message to the world that we need not fear the victims of this crisis. After that meeting, the US Congress passed a bill that committed $15 billion to help fight the spread of the HIV/AIDS pandemic. In 2016, Princess became the first publicly HIV-positive lawmaker in Africa when she was elected a Member of Parliament in Zambia's National Assembly where she still serves today.[5]

Over one hundred people from urban and suburban churches across Chicago had life-changing experiences with us in Zambia. Our stories then engaged whole church congregations, and Christ sent those congregations into the world by engaging their prayers and their gifts to transform the world.

Jesus sent the Wiseguys into the world. He sent Bishop Smith's Apostolic Faith Church into the world as it demonstrated great leadership among Chicago churches in the fight against HIV and AIDS. They also sponsored water wells in Africa and helped thousands of children in Zambia and the Democratic Republic of Congo receive better health care, nutrition, and education.

Chuck Brewer, once frustrated by the ministry options offered by his church, made an enormous impact in Zambia, right in the heart of the HIV/AIDS crisis. Jesus sent Jim Reid first into Chicago and then, with his wife, Tedde, into the world to fall in love with the people of Zambia, Nicaragua, and beyond. Jim and Tedde joined the board of Living Water International and Jim served as its chair for five years. Jesus continues to send many people into the world through the work of World Vision, Living Water International, and other ministries.

Jesus sends each one of us into the world. In Chicago, we got there by using Appreciative Inquiry to collect the voices of a broad set of stakeholders and by prayerful discernment to listen and take action on what we heard. It was painful sometimes, but it enabled us to see and do what was previously invisible and apparently impossible.

None of this would have ever happened if not for a small but diverse group of Black, Brown, and White Pentecostal, Presbyterian, Lutheran, and Catholic women and men who got together to pray and to act. I still shake my head and smile as I recall how I kept second-guessing God's call for us to engage the HIV/AIDS crisis throughout our planning process. I am delighted that we chose to respect the process, and once our direction was validated by the communion of the saints, we stuck with it. The Black church did initiate our strategy coming out of The Forum in New York. Bishop Dr. Smith did bring life and light through churches and medical professionals. ARVs did become available and affordable to low-income people. The broader church did take a courageous stand with those affected by HIV/AIDS, and the ripple effect of having asked God to guide our steps at home, among our neighbors, and even to the ends of the earth continues.

Reflect

"As you sent me into the world," Jesus tells his Father, "I have sent them into the world," (John 17:18). In what way do you think God has sent you into the world? How have you or how has your church been affected by new or different voices in the world?

Write

What have you learned from your expanded circle of dialogue and how could it be applied to an even larger vision?

Share

Talk with your expanded circle about how your church might be called to change the world.

PART THREE

TO THE
ENDS OF
THE EARTH

GOD'S VISION IS TOO BIG TO SEE

As the heavens are higher than the earth,
so are my ways higher than your ways
and my thoughts than your thoughts.

ISAIAH 55:9

I N PART ONE, "You Will Be My Witnesses," we reflected on the Father's *advance directive* of his written word, his *love* we seek to practice, our *faith* which will inevitably be tested, and the hope made possible by the *gift* of the Holy Spirit. In part two, "In Jerusalem, and in All Judea and Samaria," we reflected on the *family* that formed us, and the one for which we were formed, and on the outward expanding circles of living out our faith in the context of *community, city,* and the *world.* Part three, "To the Ends of the Earth," is my journey around the world to discover how God is doing extraordinary things through ordinary people like you and me and ordinary churches like yours and mine. This final section offers more evidence that while God's vision is too big to see in the moment, he is active through his church far and near.

As you've considered each of the previous eight reflections, perhaps God's involvement in your life and that of your church is becoming clearer, or perhaps you're still searching for more evidence that he has roles for each of us in his vision for the world. It is often the case that we cannot see God's big vision for our lives because it is too big for us to see in the moment. In this reflection, I share how God wove the story of my shattered and repaired life together with that of Living Water International cofounder Gary Evans, which only became visible in hindsight.

To remind myself of the beauty of brokenness in God's hands, I keep a *kintsugi* ceramic cup on my desk. *Kintsugi* is a Japanese art form where the artist repairs a broken vessel using lacquer and pure gold to enhance its beauty. Sometimes God is at work refining and equipping *us*, sometimes he is preparing someone *else*; most of the time, he is doing both at the same time. We may also have to wait for his alignment or for other preparations to be completed before forward movement becomes visible. As we look for signs and then meditate on the complexity of God's activity in and through our lives, our confidence grows that God has a plan that we can trust.

As you read this story, I invite you to think of a time in your life when things made more sense in retrospect, but at the time you could not see what God was preparing you for.

ıııııııııııııııııııııı

In 1986, my predecessor and current colleague at Living Water International, Gary Evans, started the commercial contracting business that would make him very wealthy . . . for a while. I didn't know Gary at the time. I wouldn't meet him for another couple of decades. Today, neither of us can imagine what our life would be like if God had not been at work in the other's life decades before we met.

The year 1986 was my first full year of work inside the world Tom Monaghan built around Domino's Pizza. Both Gary and I were learning business and social skills that would one day complement the other's and ultimately God's vision. Each of us was also learning about money, the world, and what really matters in life. I was privileged to experience wealth by gaining a little bit of access to Tom's world: his helicopter, jet, golf resort, cars, the sports team he owned, and the celebrities he attracted. Gary experienced the same by collecting a few toys of his own.

Like me, Gary recalls a disrupted childhood. Mine was cut short by my dad's decision that I go to work at the age of six. Gary's childhood was derailed by his parents' divorce when he was seven. For years afterward, Gary and his brother were passed from one family member to another as their mom recovered from a nervous breakdown. Once he was older, Gary learned about business from his father, just as I did from mine. For me it was the irrigation business, and for Gary, construction.

After fifteen years working for his father's company, Evans Construction, Gary launched his own commercial contracting business, Masters Construction Services (MCS), which prospered. Gary landed a $100-million contract to build a Compaq computer facility, and life was good. He earned a pilot's license, flew airplanes for fun, and piloted a helicopter to work from a helipad atop his garage. His wife, Sharon, drove Porsches and played lots of tennis. They enjoyed a ski vacation home in Vail, a beach condo in Galveston, and a getaway home on Lake Travis. They were active in their church, where Gary was a deacon, and they were generous. They made their vacation homes available to missionaries on retreat. They hosted a woman suffering from a rare bone disease along with her family in their beach condo while she had a series of surgeries. Gary sat on the boards of various ministries, some of whose missionaries he supported financially. It was clear to them that God had given the Evanses the gift of money, and that part of their role in God's kingdom was to support it financially. He and Sharon set a goal of giving away $10 million of their own money within their lifetime to advance God's kingdom.

Like me, Gary had a life-changing experience on a mission trip to Africa. Unlike me, Gary had no interest whatsoever in going to Africa. In 1987, when chain-smoking, swearing, Jesus-loving Max asked me to go to Senegal with him, I was excited about the adventure. In 1990, when Pastor Fenton Moorhead asked Gary to go to Kenya and install roofs on mud churches, Gary responded with an alternative. He suggested that he pack up a container with roofs and ship them. Fenton clarified that the plan was to go to Africa and install these roofs themselves alongside the people those roofs would benefit, and to preach the good news of Jesus Christ.

Fenton, who was senior pastor of Sugar Creek Baptist Church in Sugar Land, Texas, had also called on another handy man in his congregation, Harry Westmoreland. Harry was the founder and owner of a drill bit manufacturing and repair shop called Lone Star Bit. He wore overalls, rode a Harley, and had calloused hands and a wide smile that made his eyes squint. He was also active at Sugar Creek as a deacon and had a passion for ministry. Domestically, he volunteered at a prison where he taught inmates to weld. Internationally, he helped a missionary in Peru drill water wells, so he was aware of the transformative power of safe drinking water. His business was born out of the oil field, and he was always around drill rigs, so he naturally told Pastor Fenton he wanted to go to Kenya with him to drill a water well. With Harry on the well, Fenton really hoped he could count on Gary's construction expertise for the roof-building project.

Gary had a business to run, and MCS was at the height of its prosperity. Besides, Gary was certain that his role in God's work was to earn money and give a portion of it away. Although he had little interest in Africa at the time, he was interested in listening to God. What God told him was in the form of a question: *Don't you want to see what you're running from?*

Gary considered this to be a reasonable thing for God to ask. What harm could come from just *seeing*? So Gary, Sharon, and their son

Gary Lynn joined Harry and JoAnn Westmoreland, their daughter Alice, and thirty more volunteers from church on a trip to Kenya.

Sharon says she was immediately struck by the *reality* of what she saw. She knew that extreme poverty existed. She had seen it on television—but this was different. Being there made it feel real in a whole new way that she would never again be able to ignore.

The medical team that traveled with them was overwhelmed by the endless need, especially in the form of waterborne illness. Day after day, doctors prescribed medication for amoebas and parasites, and people had no choice but to wash them down with the very water that made them sick. The scene was disheartening, and the need was overwhelming. They also observed that people felt cared for and loved, and they saw great value in that.

They could see that a water well was what people there really needed, but Harry's small, light drill rig was stuck in customs. As the week ended and the team prepared to return to the United States, Harry and Gary stayed behind to drill the first well after Harry and fellow team member Malcolm Morris got the drill rig out of customs. With only forty-eight hours left, they had their rig and started drilling.

When you drill with a mud rotary rig, you mix sacks of powdered bentonite clay in water to create drilling mud. This mud circulates down the hole, then back up the hole, lifting the material you've drilled out of the hole. Drilling mud also stabilizes the walls of the hole with a thin layer of clay to keep it from collapsing. Drilling through unfamiliar geology, they ran out of bentonite, scrambled to find more, and continued drilling, working every available hour, praying they would hit water before they left. Six hours before their flight departed from Nairobi, they had not hit water, and they still needed to get to Mombasa to catch a flight to Nairobi.

Harry and Gary reached their terminal in Nairobi just as the airline was closing the door on their departing flight. The close call was exhilarating, but it would have been even more exhilarating to complete that well. When they got back to Texas, Gary called his friend Gary Loveless to tell him about their adventure. Loveless, an oil man, listened to their drilling story with great interest. Gary Evans said he and Harry were going back to Kenya to finish drilling that well, and he asked Gary Loveless to join them.

"You are kidding me, right?" Gary Loveless replied.

Several weeks later, Harry and both Garys were on a plane to Mombasa. One morning in their rural drill camp, Gary Loveless noticed something peculiar about Harry.

"Harry," Gary asked, "why do you sleep with your boots on?"

"Because when the lion comes," Harry said, "you'll be looking for your boots!"

That was typical Harry Westmoreland wisdom. "When the lion attacks," he would counsel first-time visitors, "you don't have to be the fastest runner . . . you just can't be the slowest."

The team drilled a dry hole, "a post hole," Harry called it. They moved the rig, tried again, and this time the well produced nothing but saltwater. Then they drilled another post hole. Three times their hopes were high, and three times their hopes were dashed, but the heartache of it all only reinforced their commitment to find clean water for those in need. In the midst of their disappointment, they were inspired to start a nonprofit and keep trying. Gary Evans suggested they name it "Living Water International" to acknowledge both the physical and spiritual needs they intended to address.

One day on that trip, as they scoured nearby towns looking for desperately needed drilling materials required for a successful water well, they stumbled on a Jaswell J3500 drill rig. It was a rusty mess, but it still had some life in it. Upon investigation, they learned that it belonged to the oil company Amoco. By another miracle, cofounder Gary Loveless knew the people who could sell it to them, and he negotiated an impossible deal. Living Water International had its first real commercial drill rig.

Figure 9.1. The old Jaswell J3500 (left) and a current Living Water International drill rig (right)

Between 1990 and 1993, my final couple of years at Domino's and my first few at World Vision, Living Water International operated as a group of businessmen who kicked in a few thousand dollars every six months or so to send Harry to Kenya to drill on a volunteer basis. Trip after trip, Harry had drilled postholes or saltwater wells, or he wrestled with customs or equipment. Finally, in 1994, the board sent Harry to Kenya one last time saying that if he did not drill a successful well, the Living Water International experiment would be over.

On that trip, Harry decided to train a Kenyan driller rather than drill the well himself. For six weeks they worked together, Harry hoping this was the first of dozens or even hundreds of wells his Kenyan protégé would drill. But as they reached their last thirty-foot piece of drill stem, they had not hit water. Coming to terms with the possibility that Living Water International could be defunct, Harry looked to Scripture for inspiration:

> Let us not become weary in doing good, for at the proper time we will reap a harvest if we do not give up. Therefore, as we have opportunity, let us do good to all people, especially to those who belong to the family of believers. (Galatians 6:9-10)

Harry connected his last thirty-foot section of drill stem to that Jaswell J3500, asking for God's favor as they continued. Fourteen feet later, they hit water. For the first time, Harry got to develop a well in Africa. The well development process is one in which you inject compressed air down the hole to blast out all the drilling mud and silt. Eventually you end up with clear water shooting out forty feet into the air. Children danced under the artificial rain, everyone shouting for joy. I imagine Harry felt a lot like I did on my first visit to Senegal, or perhaps even better, knowing he had been used by God to provide water for this community and to save Living Water International.

In the meantime, in December 1990, Gary Evans's company suffered a devastating blow. The country had entered a recession in July of 1990 and Compaq realized they had been overbuilding, so they halted construction. The bottom fell out of the basket where Gary had put all his eggs, forcing him to lay off 450 employees. He kept thirty engineers on staff, paying them out of his pocket as he worked on the resurrection of MCS. When it had still not come to pass three years later, MCS went out of business. Gary considered joining his brother in a custom homebuilding business they had set up, but the housing industry was also on the rocks, so he took a job running a concrete manufacturing company called Precast Services outside San Antonio. He was miserable.

Since Gary and Sharon had gone on that first mission trip to Kenya in 1990, their annual income had plummeted, and they struggled to adjust their lifestyle. They sold their vacation properties in a suffering real estate market, Sharon parted with her cars, and they even lost their health insurance. After eighteen years of not needing to work outside the home, Sharon took a job at their church to make ends meet.

In August 1995, Gary left Precast Services, and in November, cofounders Pastor Fenton and his wife, Mary, went to Kenya to see the work of Living Water International. Five years after its founding trip, Living Water had drilled five successful wells, but none had provided drinking water to anyone because they had no pumps or electricity. Concerned that the church's support had nothing to show for it, Fenton asked Gary to go to Kenya to see what needed to be done to operationalize those wells.

In January 1996, Gary went to Kenya for three weeks, got water flowing at two schools, and assessed the other three Living Water wells. When he reported his findings to the board in February, they hired him as Living Water International's founding executive director.

"Train, consult, and equip" became the philosophy as Living Water International began to define itself under Gary's leadership. Living Water International was cofounded by an unlikely group of people, and each of them have amazing stories to share of how they were compelled to contribute in various ways. Cofounder Larry Laird gave Gary a ten-by-ten office at his company, LEM Construction. Larry and his wife, Rosemary, also turned their catch-and-release bass fishing resort into a volunteer-run water-well drilling camp. The camp attracted missionaries that Living Water trained to drill with cofounder Harry Westmoreland's rig. Cofounders Malcom and Becky Morris continue to engage their vast professional and personal networks to passionately invite everyone they know to join the efforts.

For its first decade, 1990–2000, Living Water International focused on installing individual community water systems to offer "a cup of water in Jesus' name," which became the ministry's tagline. Partnering with local churches, drill camp alumni would drill a well and proclaim the gospel during the weeks or months it took to complete a well, then they were off to the next thirsty community.

Meanwhile in Chicago, I was learning how things work from the inside of one of the world's largest Christian relief and development agencies. I was learning about the worlds within our cities and how to connect people across the lines that divide us—among cultures, classes, geographies, and denominations. I was learning how to build a team, set goals, and harness talent and passion. I was learning about international development work and how to get things done on a global level. I earned a PhD in Organization Development at Benedictine University and learned how to use tools for corporate transformation from my mentors at Case Western Reserve, at Benedictine, and in Chicago. I practiced adapting organizational development processes for collective spiritual discernment. Every step of the way, God was preparing me for a role in something that was not yet visible to me.

Gary, meanwhile, laid everything he learned in business at the feet of the Lord. He put his experience managing projects to use providing safe, clean drinking water to people in need, but that was the easier part of his new job. The harder part was shifting from being on the giving end of ministry to the receiving end. He used to sponsor missionaries; now he was responsible for raising his own salary as well as the ministry's annual budget. It was humbling at first, but God had equipped Gary to sell projects for profit, so he now put that gift to use on behalf of others. On one of his trips to southern Sudan, Gary saw a missionary's tombstone that read simply, "He preached unto them Jesus."

Figure 9.2. A cup of water in Jesus' name

Through the simplicity and clarity of those five words, God spoke to Gary, asking him what he wanted on his tombstone.

"He gave a cup of water in Jesus' name," Gary responded, and he never looked back. From that moment on, his life was dedicated to one thing: offering a cup of water in Jesus' name. As he did that, he began to notice how God was already at work around the world. He started making partnerships with denominational organizations and national church-planting networks. Living Water International started equipping churches to more effectively proclaim the gospel and began to add hygiene and sanitation education to water-access work as Living Water grew each year under Gary's leadership.

Meanwhile in Chicago, I had a big decision to make. Fifteen years had passed since I left Domino's for a three-year tithe on my professional life. Every three years after that I had gone through a personal discernment process to decide if I would go "back to work" or renew my tithe again. I had done that five times now and decided that this time my decision process would be different. I discarded all my little deals with God and told him that my whole life was his. I was ready to commit to whatever task the Master Strategist assigned me, so I assembled a team of advisers from the Wiseguys, family, and friends to help me discern what that assignment would be. This team agreed to meet with me once a month to help sort out who I had become and what could be next for me. We narrowed it down to four options: (1) stay with World Vision where I had opportunities; (2) go back to for-profit work and pursue my fortune; (3) build a business around the consulting I was doing with friend and mentor Jim Ludema; or (4) lead a nonprofit somewhere and see if I could make a bigger difference with a smaller organization.

Discussing those options in our monthly meetings, we came to several conclusions. The team pointed out that my aptitudes, study, and skills were suited for executive-level leadership, but that it was unlikely I would ever be president of World Vision. The organization was under the excellent leadership of Rich Stearns, and whenever he left, they were not likely to fill the position from within. The team said I should consider whether or not I would feel fulfilled bumping against a ceiling for the rest of my career.

A financial adviser on the team suggested I had lost the appetite to acquire wealth. He told me I was not going to make the sacrifices required to focus on accumulating money. After sixteen years in the nonprofit sector, I knew he was right, but that did not make the fact easy to hear.

The team pointed out that I was a spiritual person. They said I was always talking about God and organizing people around God's will, so whatever I did had to take my spirituality into account.

At one of our monthly meetings, the team told me, "Mike, you should lead a Christian nonprofit that works in water."

"I know of an organization in Texas," offered another adviser, who ran an executive search firm. "They're hiring a fundraiser . . . but what they need is a CEO."

I flew to Texas to meet Gary Evans and liked him right away. His visionary exuberance reminded me of Tom Monaghan. He seemed happy to meet me too. He said he had considered more than a hundred candidates in his search for a Senior Vice President of Development, but not one seemed a good match until he met me. I told him I was honored, but I was really only interested in the job if it was a path to the role of CEO. Gary shared that, having seen several ministries die with their founders in the 1990s, he had been thinking about his succession for years. He told me his real hope in hiring a fundraiser was to find a successor, and he was interested in seeing if I was the one.

When I started working at Living Water International, the organization was like an overinflated balloon, ready to pop in any direction. With his entrepreneurial spirit, sharp mind, great instincts, faith, and courage, Gary had shepherded an impressive ministry, the growth of which was beginning to outpace its structure. Living Water hit its first

$1 million year in 2000, five years after Gary took the driver's seat. Eight years later, when I met him, the organization had grown by 800 percent. There were lines of people outside Gary's office asking him to make decisions, and the phone was ringing off the hook. Interventions around the world varied as the drill camp alumni became partners, and each partnership had its own unique agreements, standards, procedures, and equipment. It was a fantastic ministry doing great work, but it was ready for a different skillset than that of a pioneering founder—and God had been equipping me with that skillset all my life.

I've heard Gary say he became the founding executive director of Living Water International because he was the only unemployed guy at the January 1996 board meeting. I don't believe that. We both know—though Gary couldn't always see it—that God had been preparing him all along for his unique role in God's work. During his years of wealth and financial opportunity, God was showing Gary that expensive toys would never offer the deep satisfaction to be found in doing the Lord's work. Gary says he was on the job for six months at Living Water before he realized that his heartbreaking business losses were God forcing him to scale down his lifestyle so he could receive his assignment. His experience as an entrepreneur, businessman, salesman, and project manager uniquely prepared him to accept God's assignment. Gary's big dream for himself was to give away $10 million to advance God's kingdom, but that dream was too small. Gary has now played a part in mobilizing more than $350 million to advance God's kingdom, and the best is yet to come. God's dream was too big for Gary—or any human—to see. It still is.

"As the heavens are higher than the earth," wrote the prophet in Isaiah 55:9, "so are my ways higher than your ways and my thoughts than your thoughts."

God had, of course, also been preparing me all along for a vision that was too big for me to see. In this story you saw just a few of the ways God was working in my life and in Gary's to bring us together as part of something bigger than either of us could imagine. I have only shared a tiny fraction of all the ways God prepared our two stories to be woven together with those of dozens of board members, hundreds of churches, thousands of short-term trip participants and donors, and over six million formerly thirsty people.

If you have ever felt like you cannot see how you could be a part of God's redemptive plan, that's okay. We should expect that, because

God is always preparing us to participate in a vision too big for us to see. Like the *kintsugi* artist repairs the broken Japanese ceramic cup, our merciful Creator seeks to repair us for his use, and the scar tissue becomes not only beautiful but also strong. Even if it looks like your life is a mess, even if you have an addiction, or you're not the parent you wish you were, or you don't have the

Figure 9.3. A *kintsugi* cup: beautiful in its brokenness

job you wish you had, or any job at all, God wants to work through you to redeem the world.

Whatever the circumstance, God is preparing you to participate in a redemptive vision that you cannot see right now. There are other people involved in that vision, and God is preparing them too.

God can and will lead the way forward, and as you follow, the right lives will come together in God's perfect timing. Perhaps one day you will help others who are suffering the way you are right now, and your capacity to identify with their pain will be exactly what they need. Or maybe the skills you learned in that job you despise will be exactly what you need for the assignment God will give you when the time is right.

God's ways are always bigger. God's thoughts are always bigger. God is at work in your life whether you can see it or not. In fact, it is likely that you can't see it, because God's vision is too big for us to see.

Reflect

Recall some of the significant people and events in your life from the past that prepared you to take an important step forward—a mentor, a failure, a passion, or an open door.

Write

Record a story of a time when you thought things were not working out according to your plan, but in retrospect, things were indeed working out according to God's plan.

Share

Share a story of God's ways being bigger than yours.

GOD IS ALREADY AT WORK IN THE CHURCH THERE

I have other sheep that are not of this sheep pen.
I must bring them also.
They too will listen to my voice,
and there shall be one flock
and one shepherd.

JOHN 10:16

SOMETIMES, WE CHRISTIANS speak of the gospel as if it is something we "bring" to distant lands. This has certainly been the model for hundreds of years and may still be for some people groups even today. A complementary model considers that since the Creator and Sustainer of all creation is *already at work everywhere,* we might also identify how God is at work in distant lands and come alongside that work to support it. This approach also enables us to learn from God's activity and even "import" what God is doing in other parts of the world into our own communities, churches, and organizations.

Up to this point we have been looking at concentric rings that expand outward from self to family, church, community, city, and world, or "to the ends of the earth." Through these reflections, I hope you will begin to see that someone else's "there" could be your "here."

For people in other parts of the world, the ends of the earth might be the United States of America. In this reflection, the concentric circles of influence emanating from other locations have significantly influenced our work here at Living Water International.

A Pew Research Center report titled *The Future of World Religions* predicts that between 2010 and 2050, the portion of the world's population that is Christian is expected to remain steady at 31 percent, though where those Christians live is expected to shift from North America and Europe to Sub-Saharan Africa. In fact, Sub-Saharan Africa is projected to become the region of the world with the largest number of Christians, rising from 24 percent in 2010 to 38 percent in 2050—all the more reason to learn how God is at work in the church "there."[1]

As you read these stories, I invite you to consider how and where you have seen God working in the church there—some place other than here, either across the city or around the world.

⁣⁣⁣⁣⁣⁣⁣⁣⁣⁣⁣⁣⁣⁣⁣⁣⁣⁣⁣⁣⁣

Africa

My eyes began to open to how much we could learn from the church in Africa back when Princess Kasune Zulu showed us around Zambia. Many years later I received a master class in church mobilization for WASH (Water, Sanitation, and Hygiene) in Africa from my friends at the Evangelical Fellowship of Zimbabwe, or EFZ (pronounced E-F-Zed for Americans who want to pronounce it as they do in Zimbabwe).

EFZ has existed longer than Zimbabwe has been a country. Zimbabwe became a modern, independent nation in 1980. The body known today as EFZ was founded in 1962 with a vision to create "an alliance of evangelicals impacting the nation by obeying the Great Commission," and a mission "to mobilize, empower, and network evangelicals for the accomplishment of the Great Commission in Zimbabwe."[2]

Today EFZ consists of nine hundred member bodies including churches, denominations, ministries, and parachurch organizations representing more than 4.5 million people, roughly a quarter of Zimbabwe's population. EFZ is governed by Black African men and women who lead the country's most vibrant Christian churches, ministries, and denominations.

The history of Zimbabwe is complex, tumultuous, and not an area of my expertise. It is, however, relevant to our story to note that Great Britain colonized this land in the late nineteenth century and that it became the British colony of Southern Rhodesia, then the Federation of Rhodesia and Nyasaland, then an unrecognized state called Rhodesia before gaining independence as the Republic of Zimbabwe four decades ago.

Now fast-forward a few decades to the day my friend Greg Holder was whitewater rafting on the Zambezi River on the border of Zimbabwe and Zambia. Greg is a longtime friend of Living Water International and lead pastor of The Crossing, a church near St. Louis, Missouri. He tells the whole story in his book *Never Settle: Choices, Chain Reactions, and the Way Out of Lukewarminess,* but it is enough to know that the Zambezi ejected Greg from his raft and into a whirlpool. Gasping, swirling, he was in one of those adrenalized states where time slows down and you contemplate destinies in microseconds. It also happened to be his wedding anniversary. As the vortex pulled off his shoes below him, he imagined his wife, Robin, waiting alone at the dinner they planned that evening. Praying to God for help, he suddenly found himself back on the raft with no idea how he got there. Had the whirlpool spit him out?

Greg soon learned that his rafting guide Timba had pulled him out of the water, and he thought of a line in Exodus: "I will redeem you with an outstretched arm" (Exodus 6:6). Greg never got Zimbabwe out of his heart, and he and his board grew compelled to invest in water ministry there.

"Are you *sure* you want to do that?" I asked, trying to dissuade them. I recognized in my question the same tone I took in my World Vision days at The Storehouse when the team said they wanted to get involved in HIV/AIDS. You'd think I would have learned my lesson in Chicago, but I had good reasons for not wanting to get too involved in Zimbabwe. We were not really working there at the time, and the country was kind of a pariah state. Its politics were tumultuous, and race relations were tense. Its revolutionary government had links to communist China, so it suffered economic embargos, and it is expensive to start operations in a new country. They would get more for their money elsewhere. But nothing could dissuade The Crossing leadership from a sense that God had called them to work in Zimbabwe.

Living Water International's only Zimbabwe connection at the time was a drilling operation called Global Water Partners. We put together a package for The Crossing to fund a drill rig for Global Water Partners and sponsor some wells, and they had something to invest in as their response to God's call on their church.

All of this happened at the same time as we were engaging our global staff in a process of redefining our relationship with the global church. Our regional vice president for Africa, Dr. Zephaniah Madziakapita, was relatively new on the job. I could hear the sensitivity in his voice. He was making an effort to respect our existing relationships as he shared an idea that would go on to transform our work around the world more positively than we could imagine at the time.

"Mike, what do you think about us developing a relationship with a church network? It's called the Evangelical Fellowship of Zimbabwe, EFZ."

Zephaniah's suggestion implied a big geographical shift within the country. It might also require a significant church partner to more narrowly designate its gifts. We decided to continue supporting our existing drilling implementer but to also dip our toe in the water with a $50,000 investment through EFZ.

Years later I learned from Rev. Lindani Dube, EFZ's general secretary at the time, that at that very moment a prospective funding partner was putting conditions on grants to EFZ that its leaders felt were misaligned with their Christian convictions. Having just decided they could no longer accept this money, they were praying for something to replace it and saw our $50,000 investment as a direct response to their prayers.

Concurrently, EFZ was an answer to prayers we had been praying since our 2010 Watershed strategic planning process. In the decades before we met, EFZ had developed five commissions to accomplish its purpose. One of them was the Humanitarian Relief and Development Commission, which already had relationships with the Ministry of Environment, Water, and Climate; the Ministry of Health and Child Care; and the Ministry of Agriculture and Rural Development—exactly the friends we needed.

Leveraging all these relationships, Zephaniah worked with EFZ to develop a program they called Salt and Light, to be launched in Epworth, an impoverished settlement near the capital of Harare. They proposed training all kinds of groups to help meet their goals: water point committees, village pump minders, community health clubs, and the district development council. But it all began with a network of fifty local churches. EFZ convened the leaders of these churches to cast a vision for what God could do in the Epworth Zone if they worked together to lead a WASH program. These local leaders selected one congregation to serve as a Lead Modeling Church to assist in collecting baseline data, lead ongoing reporting activities, promote good hygiene and sanitation practices, and play a role as coordinator for the church network. The Lead Modeling Church would then train other Modeling Churches to do the same, then replicate that training among churches in its area.

The Crossing church leadership found themselves philosophically and theologically aligned with the proposal, got excited, and visited the work in Africa. They loved what they saw and increased their investment. EFZ, The Crossing, and Living Water International formed a triangle of relationships that leveraged the expertise of each and allowed for direct friendship between churches while keeping money from getting in the way of our relationships. Through this experience, Living Water International first started looking at multi-year partnerships and systematically measuring outputs not only in terms of water provision, but also sanitation infrastructure, improvements in hygiene behaviors, and the empowerment of local churches. In its first four years, the Epworth WASH program engaged the leadership of more than one hundred churches, resulting in eighty-six new sanitation and hygiene promotion activities, the rehabilitation of twenty-one existing wells, and the drilling of twenty-two new wells, serving 10,500 people. Churches began to utilize their new training and facilitation skills to address other social issues in their communities. The quality of the work was recognized by the Zimbabwe government's National Committee on WASH, which held the program up as a model to be emulated.

Cocreating and implementing the Salt and Light program with EFZ and their Humanitarian Relief and Development Commission educated us in rural African community development and church mobilization. Discovering God at work through EFZ informed our WASH Program Area (WPA) model and our approach to church mobilization. The lessons we learned by joining God's work in Zimbabwe influenced how we invite churches to transform their communities in eighteen countries. Under the thoughtful leadership of Jonathan Wiles, our senior vice president of programs, we formalized these lessons, and those learned in other countries, in a toolset we call *Flourish: Mobilizing Churches & Communities for WASH-Focused Transformation.*[3] Working with the various government ministries to which EFZ introduced us informed our *Theory of Change,* a kind of map that shows the causal links between all our

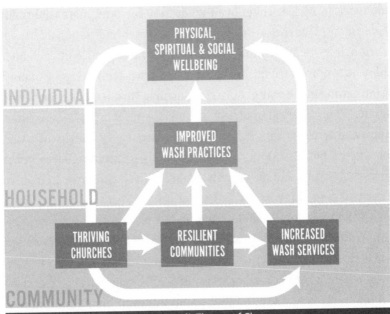

Figure 10.1. Living Water International's Theory of Change map

various programmatic activities at the household, community, district, and national levels, and our ultimate goal, which is people's increased physical, spiritual, and social wellbeing.

The relationships formed and knowledge shared among EFZ, The Crossing, and Living Water International produced a message of church unity so powerful we took it on tour as a conference, drawing rave reviews from audiences and high-ranking leaders in government and church, heads of state, and delegations from across the continent.

When we first met EFZ, they saw us as a direct answer to their prayers. EFZ soon revealed itself to be an answer to our prayers and those of the church family at The Crossing. Once again, we found ourselves participating in a vision too big for us to see, and we got there by identifying where the Master Strategist was *already* at work in the church "there" and obediently joining the adventure of coming alongside God's work to support it.

Latin America

I have Latin America to thank for my earliest intercultural exchange. My admiration for Juan Carlos's multigenerational Cuban home made a deep impact on my view of family. I credit my semester in Spain for my love for history, food, and the basics of Spanish, the "language of heaven." In my twenties and thirties, I enjoyed the vantage point of seeing the world through the experience and wisdom of Natalie's father, my friend and mentor, Reverend Juan Boonstra, host of *La Hora de la Reforma*. So it seemed natural to me that, organizationally, we have Latin America to thank for the vocabulary we use regarding the integral mission of the church.

Integral mission, or *holistic mission*, refers to the inseparable proclamation and demonstration of the gospel seen in the life and works of Jesus Christ. It comes from the Latin American term *misión integral*, coined by members of the Latin American Theological Fellowship (Fraternidad Teológica Latinoamericana, or FTL), whose work spread the concept throughout evangelicals around Latin America. In 1974, one of FTL's founders, Ecuadorian theologian René Padilla, presented the idea of *misión integral* to evangelicals from 150 countries gathered at the International Congress on World Evangelization in Lausanne, Switzerland.[4] His words inspired Christians around the world to consider that there is no biblical dichotomy between evangelism and social responsibility in helping the poor and oppressed gain access to the peace of Christ. The task, rather, is to bring all of life under the lordship of Jesus Christ.

The concept of integral mission was well received at the Congress on World Evangelization, but as civil wars raged across Central America in the 1980s, many evangelicals steered clear of social activism for its associations with liberation theology. Indeed, a number of Latin American Catholics in pursuit of legal, economic, and social justice had found allies in Marxist movements gaining momentum at the time.

During more than a decade of civil wars, many Central American evangelicals continued to keep a safe distance from social activism, often holding to a rigid, oversimplistic dichotomy between "spiritual" and "worldly" concerns. "My kingdom is not of this world," they quoted Jesus to say, and they kept their eyes on the afterlife prize . . . until the deadliest hurricane in two hundred years forced them to ask new questions.

In 1989, Hurricane Mitch left millions homeless, striking Honduras worst of all. Of the eleven thousand Central Americans killed by the hurricane, seven thousand were Hondurans. Living Water International had just established a presence in Honduras only a couple months before the hurricane struck. Its leaders at the time were a pastor and a nurse, Mike and Georgeann Gullikson, both alumni of Living Water's 1990 founding trip to Kenya. When disaster struck, Mike and Georgann had no choice but to lend a hand where God was already at work with and through his people. They were so new to Honduras they lacked the experience and language skills to initiate any work on their own, but Mike had a truck and Georgeann was a nurse, so they lent a hand as churches took action. As push came to shove in the throes of the storm, evangelical Christians no longer felt inspired to preach that Jesus' kingdom is not of this world. New Bible passages skipped to the front of the line:

- "I was hungry and you gave me something to eat" became more salient as 70 percent of Honduras' crops were destroyed, fifty thousand cattle drowned, and 60 percent of chickens were wiped out. Mike used the truck intended to support his drilling operation to deliver rice and beans to remote areas.

- "I was thirsty and you gave me something to drink" became more relevant as 70 percent of Honduras lost access to fresh water.[5]

- "I was a stranger and you invited me in," and "I needed clothes and you clothed me" took on new urgency as so many homes were destroyed that 20 percent of Hondurans were left homeless.[6]

- "I was sick and you looked after me" became church work for nurses like Georgann as health care facilities were left without electricity or water, and a large percentage of healthcare workers were themselves affected by floods and evacuated.[7]

- "I was in prison and you came to visit me" took on new meaning as an estimated 70 to 80 percent of the country's transportation network was wiped out, including most bridges and secondary roads, taking public transportation offline, and leaving people feeling trapped and dependent on visitors with vehicles, like Mike in his support truck. (Scripture excerpts are from Matthew 25:31-36.)

Living Water had also very recently begun work in El Salvador, where staff partnered with relief workers from Samaritan's Purse to help distribute emergency bio-sand water filters through connections with local churches, clinics, schools, and mayors' offices. After a few dry "postholes" drilled in the mountains with Harry Westmoreland, Living Water El Salvador's first successful wells were drilled by drill camp alumnus and missionary Paul Dařílek at schools serving as refugee centers in the Bajo Lempa River valley, where entire homes had floated into the sea with the floodwaters. After the storm, Samaritan's Purse Canada remained in relationship with Living Water, sponsoring a bio-sand water filter program helping us install thousands of household bio-sand water filters in homes that could not be served by drilled wells because the underground water is salty.

All along the coastal planes of Central America, the hand-dug wells people depended on were contaminated by floodwater. Pit latrines, chicken coops, pigsties, water wells, and the river all sloshed together in the flood before settling back down in people's open, hand-dug wells. Our drilling operations were very simple at the time. Harry Westmoreland used to joke that his portable LS-100 drill rig "could drill up to one hundred feet . . . through butter"—a big rock would stop it in its tracks.

But in certain geologies it was perfect for drilling cased, sealed water wells impervious to floodwaters, accessing deep aquifers free of superficial contamination.

Living Water International was still a young and inexperienced ministry when Hurricane Mitch struck. Thankfully, God was already at work opening eyes, some of them reluctant, to the *misión integral* of the church. God gave us the opportunity to come alongside. In El Salvador, Living Water ended up working with theologian Ruth Padilla-DeBorst, the daughter of René Padilla, in the Red de Misión Integral, or Integral Mission Network, which promoted the whole gospel vision among churches throughout El Salvador.

Figure 10.2. Handwashing with clean water at a homemade "tippy tap" in Latin America

This language about "integral mission," forged in Latin America, has permeated our strategy. It has compelled us to look closely at the relationship between our *demonstration* and *proclamation* of the gospel. As a result, we considered with our board how we could adjust our budget to better reflect our commitment to both "water and the Word" by investing more resources in gospel proclamation.

Today, under the leadership of our regional vice president for Latin America & the Caribbean, Wesley Charles from Haiti, we now see the *misión integral* of the church in action across Latin America, the Dominican Republic, and Haiti as church partners promote WASH strategies, and more recently, stand firm with their brothers and sisters in the fight for life against Covid-19, all of it *in Jesus' name*.

South Asia

When Natalie and I were newlyweds at the Word of God community, some people there believed in healing miracles, but not everyone had experienced them or embraced the possibility. Each of our traditions engaged prayer with different levels of intentionality, passion, or joy, and all of us got to learn from one another's traditions, practices, and disciplines. We are still learning from others as part of a global community today, and our South Asian friends have taught us many lessons about courage, conviction, zeal, and especially the power of prayer.

South Asia is not known for its prevalence of Christians. It is right at the center of what some missiologists call the "10/40 Window," the region between 10 and 40 degrees north of the equator where people are said to have least access to the Christian message. Yet our experience is that God is already as powerfully at work there as anywhere else in the world.

Christians are a tiny minority in South Asia today, but it is interesting to note that some of our faith's most ancient roots are in this region. According to tradition, Thomas the apostle established seven Christian churches on India's southwestern Malabar Coast in AD 52, around the same time Bartholomew was planting churches on India's northwestern Konkan Coast.[8] Crosses associated with the ancient Saint Thomas Christians have been found as far north as the land now known as Pakistan.[9] In fact, South Asian Christianity goes back to the very earliest moment of the faith—the Parthians mentioned in

Acts 2:9 as having received God's gift of the Holy Spirit on Pentecost were from present-day Afghanistan.

Because Christians are marginalized and sometimes persecuted in this part of the world, we generally do not talk publicly about our work there. For the safety of our staff and the Christians with whom they serve, I will not refer to any specific communities, regions, or even countries in the stories featured in this section. All names are selected randomly from an internet search for "South Asian baby names." But the stories are real, and we have a lot to learn from the courage, conviction, and zeal of our South Asian sisters and brothers in Christ.

Born in South Asia, Thevan moved to North America for college at the age of eighteen. For nearly twenty years after graduation, he worked as a state water quality engineer, then as a metallurgist for an oil company before God called him to return to his hometown in service of sharing the gospel. His wife started an orphanage, and Gary Evans equipped him to establish a water ministry to serve a fast-growing church-planting network in South Asia.

"Local missionaries direct us to the water needs in the rural villages they serve," Thevan says. "Before drilling begins, they ask local leaders for permission to say a prayer. Community leaders always grant permission because they want the gods on their side. Then, when that prayer is directed to Jesus, that is often the first time his name has ever been uttered in that village."

As relationships are forged, someone nearly always shares that they or one of their children is suffering from a serious health concern. Often, they have consulted local faith healers who say the root of the illness is a failure to appease a particular god. They are told what sacrifices that god requires and what they cost. Desperate for help, parents spend what little money they have on the hope of appeasing these gods. They often feel hopeless because they have been told that their eternal destiny is to spend countless reincarnations in a world governed by these unfeeling and capricious gods.

Sometimes the illness is waterborne and goes away with clean water, opening the door for conversations about health, hygiene, sanitation, water, and the living water offered by Jesus. Through these new friendships, people trapped in a cycle of appeasement are introduced to the idea that they no longer need to placate the gods by sacrificing animals. They learn the Christian belief that all the blood that ever needed to be shed was shed by Christ on the cross two thousand years ago. They are relieved to discover their life of religious striving can end by accepting God's grace and following his son, Jesus. They are encouraged to learn that they have brothers and sisters in Christ who will disciple them in their everyday relationship with Jesus. They experience joy in the belief that God is love and that we are made in God's image to love our neighbors. Finding themselves in this new story, they experience new purpose, meaning, and hope in a life to come in the eternal presence of a loving God.

Note the parallels between Thevan's world and that of first-century Christians. In both the early church and South Asia today, Christians are a minority in a polytheistic religious environment that requires sacrifices to the gods. Believers largely meet in house-churches for security, cost, and concern for the poor. Dominant religions persecute both, and Jesus-followers respond with prayer and by blessing those who curse them.

"We could never defeat the religious extremists with our strength," Thevan says. "Prayer is all we have, and it is powerful."

As he shared these stories, tensions in his country were unusually high due to political factors. Churches were being burned and pastors ousted from their pulpits. "But as persecution increases," Thevan says,

so does prayer. I am participating in a twenty-one-day fast right now as we speak. Our church has a sign-up sheet to ensure that we are praying 24/7. Prayer teams are traveling from village to village and city to city, filling them with prayer. In the past year my mother-in-law has been to every state in the country to pray for it, and we are incorporating more prayer in our office.

Because he is so thoroughly bicultural, Thevan hesitated to share another parallel between his world and that of the first century Christians—miracles.

As a Westerner, you might find this hard to believe, but in the rural villages we are seeing miracles: sick people healed, deaf people hear, the disabled walk, and mute tongues speak. [South Asian Regional Directors] Tahir and Rohan will tell you the same thing. I never saw this when I was in the United States, or even in the big cities here. I never see it among highly educated people, but in the villages, people commonly report miracles when they pray to Jesus.

Thevan's colleague 1,500 miles to the north, Tahir, is also bicultural, having studied and lived in North America for many years. "In North America," he says, "people ask why miracles are so common in the Bible and so rare today. Here it is the opposite—we see far more miracles in the world around us than we see in the New Testament."

When Living Water International's director of communications visited Tahir, they went to a church in a region where Christians make up fewer than 0.15 percent of the population.[10] After a Sunday service, he asked about the church's origin. They said it all started when an itinerant pastor named Promod prayed in Jesus' name for a woman named Nirmala who had been sick for two years. When she was healed, her husband, Kalu, enrolled in a Christian seminary and started a healing prayer ministry that turned into a church. Then the entire congregation shared miracle stories. There was a deaf and mute boy who attended church because he liked how the room made him feel. One day he shouted his first word, "Alleluia!" and his parents enrolled him in school the following semester. An ice cream vendor named

Waloo said a tumor disappeared from his throat when someone prayed for him in Jesus' name. He pointed to stretchmarks where the tumor had once been. A young woman named Romila walked for the first time after someone prayed for her in Jesus' name. The stories went on and on.

Never having seen such a thing, our communications director was incredulous. He thought surely they were just making up stories, but for the next three days Tahir took him from village to village where Christians and non-Christians alike testified that these stories were true. The testimonies were so incredible he did not know what to make of them, but he captured them and retold the stories to the broader organization.

Pastor Promod now enjoys high esteem in the communities he serves, but that was not always the case. Several years ago, walking home from a housewarming party, he was surrounded by a mob of about seventy men who demanded he stop preaching his foreign religion. They beat him and left him on the side of the road to reconsider his faith.

There were no social or political advantages to being a Christian. The only thing that compelled Promod to carry on was his personal experience of the living Christ. Not long after he was left on the side of the road, he partnered with Living Water to drill water wells offering safe drinking water in Jesus' name to the villages he served. At first the reaction was not entirely positive. Despite his clear and repeated invitation, people did not believe that the water was theirs to use for free. They assumed it was only for Christians, whom they resented because they saw them becoming more prosperous. Those who accepted the invitation spent less time hauling water; got sick less; had healthier kids and more free time; and missed fewer days of school. In a culture steeped in exclusion, it took months of persistent invitation for the Christian community to convince others that the water was theirs too. Once the community accepted that invitation,

Figure 10.3. In South Asia, "the wells became like outposts" for sharing the gospel

the reputation of the local Christians changed. They became known for their love, service, and imitation of a Lord who heals the sick.

"The wells became like outposts where I could talk to people about Jesus," Promod said. Before long he was welcome wherever he went. If anyone spoke ill of him, Christians and non-Christians alike defended him. After his demonstration of God's love by offering clean water, people were willing to listen to him proclaim the living water offered by Jesus. Most did not respond by becoming Christians themselves, but some did. More importantly, Promod and his fellow Christians can now speak and act freely—and let the Holy Spirit do the rest.

"Water is melting away persecution," Promod said, "and it is opening doors for the gospel. I used to be hated for my faith. Now I'm invited into people's homes. Now I am seen with respect."

When South Asian leaders like Thevan and Tahir interface with their counterparts from Africa and Latin America, their courage and faith become contagious and spread around the world. Conversely, the experience of their colleagues from other continents informs their work.

"We used to approach our work with the mentality that the government was always against us and always would be," Thevan says,

> but we found out that's not always true. After visiting WASH Program Areas in Africa and Latin America, we began to consider that maybe their approach could work in our country too. Applying lessons learned from Uganda and Mexico, we discovered that we offer so much value that government officials at the county- and state-level would embrace us as we support their work.

Thevan testifies that the words Latin America has given us about the integral mission of the church have given his fellow Christians a more complete understanding of the gospel. "In our culture, many Christians take pride in their distance from everyday life," Thevan says.

> Their mentality is, "You are from the world; I am from the church." Bible schools here do not teach integral mission, but when we teach it from the Flourish handbook, pastors know the Bible so well they immediately catch on. It's like a switch turns on and suddenly they have new ways to be like Jesus. "This is like a gold mine for us," church workers say. "We are the champions of the community now. We are at the forefront of community life!"

In turn, coming face-to-face with the spiritual environment of South Asia has enhanced our understanding of our work, prayer, our world, and the role of the Holy Spirit within it. As Christians from a context of relative power and wealth, many of us have never been forced to rely on the power of prayer to the extent that our South Asian colleagues have. Our work with our South Asian colleagues constantly reminds us of the spiritual dynamics at play everywhere in the world. Their courage inspires us, and our relationship with them has enriched our prayer life and generated a desire for deeper spiritual formation. Spiritual disciplines we learned from them are spreading throughout our global staff, enhancing the lives and work of a larger body.

Figure 10.4. Christians "are the champions of the community now"

Observing the taxing and arduous efforts that our South Asian colleagues are making in pursuit of God's kingdom has made us more acutely aware of the potential spiritual fatigue that many in ministry risk. We have been sensitized to the need for spiritual care and discipleship among our own staff as they reach out to others. Recently, at the invitation of a shared donor with Fuller Theological Seminary, we have initiated a program to engage our staff in spiritual formation groups so they will be better equipped for the long haul of ministry.

There is much to learn from our Christian brothers and sisters over "there," where God is already at work. In the next reflection, we will explore how God is also moving in our churches "here." Whether there or here, we have much to learn and embrace as we seek to serve the Lord through our global, twenty-first-century church.

Reflect

Identify where you draw the line between "here" and "there," and recall what you have learned from the church over "there," across town or in other countries.

Write

Record a short list of surprising discoveries you've made from some place other than your home, home church, or home neighborhood.

Share

Share with your friends which of these discoveries you would like to apply in your life or your church.

GOD IS MOVING IN THE CHURCH HERE

And through your offspring
all nations on earth will be blessed,
because you have obeyed me.

GENESIS 22:18

G OD'S OLDEST PROMISE is that "all nations on earth will be blessed" through the descendants of Abraham, the father of our faith.

I used to think that blessing all nations was about sacrifice. I thought it was about us giving a bit of our wealth to others. Now I believe that blessing all nations is about something much more exciting than that. It is about tapping into the divine, redemptive force of the Master Strategist who is at work with and through his people to redeem the world.

In my experience, churches that tap into that force flourish, while those that don't fade away before us. You may have heard the Pew Research Center's talk about the exodus of "nones" (those who check "none" under religious affiliation on a survey), who are leaving church.[1] The Barna Group, which specializes in the study of religious belief and behavior, says the number of practicing Christians in America is down to *half* of what it was in 2000.[2] I am in no position to question these findings, but I *can* tell you there is another side to the story. In fact,

I've seen both sides at my home church, Grace Presbyterian Church in Houston, Texas.

In this reflection I describe how Grace is shifting from struggling to thriving by identifying where God is already at work and joining that work. Then I tell stories of other communities across America doing the same and flourishing as a result.

And it's an adventure! In the epilogue, I invite to capture your own stories and then share them more broadly to build a growing awareness of God's amazing work through his church.

As you read these stories, I invite you to consider how God is at work "here," in people, communities, and ministries close to you.

||||||||||||||||||||||

Grace Presbyterian

Natalie and I had just moved to Houston and we needed to find a church. We laid a map on the table and drew a circle with a thirty-minute drive radius around our home. We looked at all the churches within that circle. Because of our experience at the Word of God community and our work in Chicago, Natalie and I could make ourselves at home in many of the churches we saw. But my dad lived with us, so our ideal church would be one where he felt comfortable. We also thought it would be meaningful to Natalie and me for our younger two daughters to experience a bit of our three-legged stool by learning the Heidelberg Catechism at our new church. It was a running joke in our home that our younger girls had never been catechized. "Don't blame me," our youngest daughter Katie might say. "I've never been catechized."

There aren't many Dutch people in Houston. We found only two Reformed churches of the kind we grew up in. Both were outside our thirty-minute radius, so we considered the Presbyterians, our Calvinist cousins. After a little exploration we zeroed in on Grace Presbyterian.

It was close to our home, and it was the kind of high-steeple church my dad could respect. If our girls didn't hate it, it would be a great place for them to be catechized.

Our girls hated it. They did not feel included in its youth groups and small groups. Grace was exactly the kind of church demographers tell us are in decline. It was not good at welcoming newcomers because there generally weren't very many. Later, an outside consultant would tell us the number of people who had come to faith at Grace Presbyterian in the past five years was zero. The church was held together by family tradition and denominational fidelity . . . and the denomination was in the midst of a split.

Concern with growing theological disputes had led some churches to split off and form ECO: A Covenant Order of Evangelical Presbyterians. Grace lost several members in the split, contributing to financial decline. Six months after we started attending Grace, our lead pastor resigned. Natalie and I didn't feel particularly welcomed either. Church elders knew about my work with Living Water International but made no attempt to engage me in missions. I'm sorry to say that, at the time, I was relieved to just sit in the pew to worship and to be recharged so that I could go out and change the world elsewhere.

Our daughters began to attend another nearby church, Ecclesia. We were friends of the church and its pastor Chris Seay, who is the guy I was cruising around with after Hurricane Harvey. In order to continue worshiping as a family, Natalie and I started going to Ecclesia each Saturday night with our girls, then to Grace Presbyterian each Sunday morning with their grandpa.

We attended Grace like this for about five years before Margaret Ellis, a Grace member, went on a Living Water International trip to Central America. She came home with great stories to tell and recruited a few people from church to go on another trip with her. They too came home excited and helped her as she kept working the crowd. Over the course of a few years, a group of Grace members formed who had something to be excited about.

Around that time, Grace brought back its former youth pastor, Dr. Trey Little, as its new senior pastor, hoping he might spice things up a bit. Trey had been an investment banker and a youth leader at Grace when he decided to go to seminary. He pastored a church in San Antonio before being called back home to Grace. We became fast friends when he learned about my work.

"Mike, I really have a passion for Haiti," my new pastor said. "When are you going to go with me to Haiti?"

"Whenever you want, Pastor," I said. "Why Haiti?"

Just as I had my big experience in Senegal and Living Water International founders had theirs in Kenya, Trey had a life-changing experience in Haiti in 2010, just nine days after a devastating earthquake. On that trip, he had a clear sense that God wanted him to be in relationship with people from that nation.

We put together a quick three-day trip with Living Water's visionary regional vice president, Wesley Charles, a Haitian himself, and Jack Vaughn, a volunteer from Dallas who initiated our work in Haiti in 2003. We met with the Haitian team and some of their church partners to explore the WASH Program Area (WPA) we wanted to launch and the impact it would have. Trey thought about how this could fit in with his vision for Grace as a community of people "living to make Jesus visible." He envisioned accomplishing that by becoming "a people of blessing," and "blessing people across the street and around the world." He was looking for a long-term missions opportunity to achieve those goals. Aware that he had a group of parishioners excited about going on trips, he reasoned that by defining and formalizing the relationship between Grace and Living Water, he could consolidate his missions activities, take advantage of the energy among mission trip participants, and breathe new mission life into the church. So we put together a trial proposal for a WPA in Haiti.

Meanwhile, Trey also invited me to be an elder at Grace. This was a kind of service I had managed to escape all my life because it sounded immensely boring. But you may recall my prayer at the end of reflection four, in which I reflected on God's call to be his witness in Jerusalem, and in all Judea and Samaria, and to the ends of the earth. In that prayer, I felt God tell me to stop ignoring Jerusalem—which for me meant Houston. That was exactly when Trey invited me onto his Ministry Support Team, so I had to say yes. My acceptance also put me on the budget committee, so the numbers were all visible to me, and they had been declining for decades.

"Trey," I said, "I love your strategy, but the WASH Program Area is a $4.6 million program. We don't have that kind of money."

Trey suggested we ask someone to host a group of trip alumni and tell them about the WPA. We got about fifty people together. They were all excited about their past experiences in Haiti, Guatemala, and Honduras, and we told them about our desire to build a long-term relationship in Haiti.

"And we want to fund Living Water's WPA in northern Haiti!" Trey announced. It caught me off guard.

"Well, Trey, wearing my Living Water hat, I'd like to just say 'thank you,'" I said. "But wearing my Grace elder hat, I have to tell you, 'We do not have that kind of money.'"

"Well," Trey said, "if we get something together, can you give Grace first dibs?"

I chuckled. There was no financial risk in giving our church "dibs," so I said, "Yes, we can have first dibs." Besides, I had seen miracles happen before!

Grace could barely afford to keep a roof over our heads at the time. Bills had been stacking up during those years of having no pastor, then an interim pastor, then a new pastor. We had been neglecting a lot of maintenance during the years of denominational split, declining attendance, and diminishing resources. We made a budget to replace the church's roof, change the carpets, do some essential maintenance, and make the church more welcoming, and our total was about $5 million. That was a lot of money, but we also needed to strengthen our intention to "make Jesus visible across the street and around the world," so the elders added a 20 percent missions component to the budget to bless people in Houston's Westside neighborhood through a partner ministry, Attack Poverty, and to kick off the WPA in Haiti with close to a million-dollar start-up investment.

"We asked ourselves," Trey said, addressing a gathering of Houston church leaders a couple years later, "'How can we deepen our relationships in Haiti and have a greater long-term impact?' That's when we decided to invest in Living Water's WPA in Plaine-du-Nord, Haiti, committing to funding projects in that region for the next five years."

He pointed out that far from draining finances,

the shared passion to help the thirsty brought us together as a church. Now when we pray for the people of Haiti, we remember the names of the communities we visited, or the sisters and brothers we've served alongside. Our whole congregation got caught up in the vision of being people of blessing.

People kept going on trips, sometimes with their pastors and sometimes without them.

"As a pastor," Trey says of his first trip with his congregants, "it was inspiring to see how that trip changed the lives of everyone on that team. They couldn't wait to tell their friends and neighbors about their experience, and word quickly spread."

Our church came alive. Over time, trip alumni grew to about one hundred, and they were a constant source of energy. They were not just excited about missions or a certain budget line item. They were excited about our church making Jesus visible across the street and around the world.

"Our partnership is about so much more than participating in short term trips," Trey says. "It's about discipleship. Partnering with Living Water is not just a way to offer water to the world out there but a way to disciple our congregation here."

Figure 11.1. People kept going on trips . . . our church came alive

Trey and his whole congregation now had a vision too big to contain within the walls of Grace Presbyterian.

"To reach as many people as possible in Plaine-du-Nord with safe water and the gospel message," Trey says,

we knew we couldn't do it alone. The vision had to be bigger than any one church, so we reached out to churches across Texas and encouraged them to join us in our mission to save and transform lives. It's been so cool for me to witness how God is using this big audacious vision of partnering with churches in Haiti through Living Water to transform lives and compel the people of Grace to be courageous disciples. Changing the world is big, and man, it's so exciting to be a part of because ultimately, we believe it's not just the people of Haiti who are thirsty. "Blessed are those who hunger and thirst for righteousness, for they will be filled," Jesus said. We all need to be fed. We all need our thirst quenched.

We all have opportunities to extend grace to others. Don't underestimate what God can do when you open up to his leading.

Natalie and I had joined a Grace Presbyterian Church where a significant missions gift would have seemed impossible. After our church came alive, it seemed inevitable. Beginning with Margaret, then everyone she recruited, then a pastor's deep affection for Haiti, then continuing through life-changing experiences for over a hundred church members, Grace Presbyterian identified where God was at work in people's hearts and lives, molded its programs and budget to support that work, and became alive.

"Give yourself the time to see the results of making Jesus visible," Trey encourages other pastors. "Give your people a chance not just to *give*, but to *go*. Offer them an experience of seeing what God is doing in and through the church globally. I am convinced that the church is made for these kinds of relationships. We are made to be one Body in Christ."

To this day our younger two girls are still not catechized. Natalie and I will have to wait for our grandchildren to realize that goal, which is a whole lot easier knowing that we all belong to communities committed to finding God at work and joining in.

Sugar Creek Baptist Church

Sugar Creek Baptist Church, founded in 1979 and host of Living Water's original mission trip, is the heir and benefactor of a century-long heritage of missions zeal.

In 1903, the Texas Baptist Convention invited the charismatic Dr. Livingston T. Mays from Nashville to preach at a series of Houston tent revivals. In the midst of those services, Mays was called to pastor a yet-to-be-founded church on the south edge of town, and South Main Baptist Church has been known for its mission zeal ever since. One of its many ministry efforts was a church plant in Sugar Land, Texas, the Imperial Sugar company town that became the affluent home to country clubs and golf courses.

Sugar Creek's early pastor, Dr. J. Dalton Havard, had degrees from Southwestern Baptist Theological Seminary and Baylor University, but he was a small-town guy from Lufkin at heart and nervous about his calling.

"I was actually afraid to do it," he remembered, "I had never pastored in an affluent area like Sugar Land, but the Lord seemed to say to me, 'Look, those people put their britches on one leg at a time just like everybody else, and they have the same needs!'"[3]

Thus reassured, Dr. Havard continued the mission zeal of the church's founders by spending three evenings a week knocking on doors to invite neighbors to visit Sugar Creek.

Pastor Fenton Moorhead assumed leadership at Sugar Creek in 1989. A key figure in South Florida's Jesus Movement in the early 1970s, Fenton embodied mission zeal. In addition to leading Sugar Creek, he cofounded Living Water International and various other ministries such as Urban Camps for at-risk inner-city youth and the Second Mile Mission Center, which meets local training and education needs. He helped start the Set Free Alliance and the Child Freedom Coalition, both of which rescue and care for enslaved, orphaned, and vulnerable children in South Asia. Altogether, he helped start more than sixty mission churches and supported many other local and global ministries from Kenya to Kyrgyzstan.

When Dr. Mark Hartman became lead pastor at Sugar Creek Baptist Church, he joined almost four thousand members with a passion for missions and led the team through years of exponential growth. A few years into his tenure, Pastor Mark reached out to me, not because his church needed missions support, but because he recognized that our ministries had always been a part of one another, and he wanted to help Living Water serve the broader church.

Valuing his wisdom and experience, I immediately invited Dr. Hartman to participate in our Watershed strategic planning process, and he made a critical contribution to our relationship with the church by volunteering to help think through our strategy from the perspective of a church leader. We had been working on strategy for a couple days when Mark and I found ourselves on a break together.

"Mike, where is the church in this strategy?" he asked me.

"Pastor Mark," I said, "the church is all over this strategy. It's part of our mission, 'water and the Word'; this is all about the church."

"That's interesting," Mark said with his supportive smile, "then why don't we ever use the words *the church* in the strategy documents?"

I looked all over the plans and documents we had been creating and was shocked to discover he was right. We never actually used the words *the church* in our written documents.

Awakened and enlightened by the conversation, we began adjusting our language and asked Pastor Mark to join our board of directors as chairman of the Spiritual Emphasis Committee. In 2013, Dr. Hartman

Figure 11.2. The church is at the center of Living Water International's WASH strategy

and his team of board members and staff drafted our formative *Mobilizing the Church* document. They drew from sector peers, local and international church leaders, experience with the Salt and Light program, as well as Living Water's Church Mobilization Forums in Ghana and Zimbabwe to outline how we serve the church globally and domestically and how we bridge the two together.

Today Sugar Creek Baptist Church is a diverse and thriving community with more than twelve thousand members who meet on four campuses. Their congregants come from over ninety countries of birth, speak more than seventy non-English languages at home, and their mission zeal is felt in their community, seven different Texas prisons, numerous ministries like ours, and countries around the world.

Advent Conspiracy

More than a decade ago three church leaders—Greg Holder, Chris Seay, and Rick McKinley—found themselves pondering what a dreadful time of year Christmas is for a pastor. They put it this way in their book *Advent Conspiracy*:

> Several years ago, a few of us were lamenting how we'd come to the end of an Advent season exhausted and sensing we'd missed it again: the awe-inducing, soul-satisfying mystery of the Incarnation. No wonder there was a dread at the beginning of each new season as we prepared to proclaim, celebrate, and worship around the story of God entering our world as one of us. Something was just not right. Along with our congregations, a creeping kind of idolatry was consuming us.
>
> We were drowning in a sea of financial debt and endless lists of gifts to buy. We had believed the marketing lie that the spending of money is the best way to express love and, in true American fashion, "more must be better." (Such a tale is still convincing enough to make "believers" out of non-Christians and Christians alike.)

It was in that moment of brutal honesty that we admitted our fear: on Christmas day, God would come near—as he always does and always is—and we would miss it yet again.

So we decided to try an experiment: What if, instead of acting like bystanders to the nativity, we led our congregations into the nativity story as participants?

We didn't know what to expect, but we knew we needed to reclaim the story of Christmas, the foundational narrative of the church. As we strove to see the birth of Christ from inside the stable instead of inside the mall, our holiday practices began to change.[4]

WORSHIP FULLY   SPEND LESS   GIVE MORE   LOVE ALL

Figure 11.3. Pillars of Advent Conspiracy

Rick, Chris and Greg identified four ideas around the celebration of Advent that they believed could change the world and made them the four pillars of Advent at their churches.

Worship Fully. From shepherds, to Persian Magi, to Mary's beautiful Magnificat, Christmas began with worship, so it should end with worship too. Let's worship Jesus *fully*, honoring him in the ways we spend our time, energy, and money, as well as in what we believe and say.

Spend Less. We all know that mindless consumption is not what Jesus wants. Let's thoughtfully evaluate the companies and causes we support with our purchases. Let's consider whether or not our spending is in line with the kinds of things Jesus cares about.

Give More. The first Christmas gift was the relational gift of God offering himself to us through Jesus. Let's also figure out ways to give relationally. Often our best gifts involve time, energy, and thought rather than money. Often our best gifts are not presents but *presence.*

Love All. Let's celebrate Christmas by loving others as Jesus has loved us. Let's offer the least of our brothers and sisters the gifts Jesus asked for: food for the hungry, water for the thirsty, hospitality to the stranger, clothes for the naked, healing for the sick, and company for the imprisoned.

They called the movement the Advent Conspiracy. Children were the first to catch on. They immediately saw that it was absurd to show up at a birthday party with gifts for everyone but the birthday boy. Yet that was exactly how the grownups had taught them to celebrate Jesus' birthday. Kids were delighted to forego gifts to celebrate Jesus. They redirected gifts and allowances, dumped change into offering plates, and their parents followed suit. Before long the original participating churches in the first Advent Conspiracy had raised half a million dollars!

They used their offering to drill water wells in refugee settlements for victims of the recently ended Liberian civil war. They visited that country, made friends, took photos, shot videos, and shared them with their congregations back home. Christmas had now become so deeply meaningful they just had to share it with others. Their Advent Conspiracy promo video went viral in the heyday of viral videos. The movement was featured on CNN, Fox, in the *Christian Post, Forbes,* and *USA Today*. Whoopi Goldberg mentioned the Advent Conspiracy on The View, and it was featured on several other media outlets.[5]

Before long, there were Advent Conspirators on every continent. People wrote in from countries as diverse as Saudi Arabia, Botswana, Mexico, China, Ukraine, Israel, Japan, Thailand, and Tanzania to share how they had conspired to make Christmas meaningful.[6] This internet phenomenon of a tool for planetary collaboration among members of the body of Christ was a harbinger of things to come.

The Advent Conspiracy is still alive today, and they don't want your money. In fact, there is no Advent Conspiracy organization to send money to if you wanted to. The conspiracy's only aim is to help you more meaningfully celebrate Christmas. Through it, countless churches have demonstrated that Christmas can still change the world through a number of great ministries. Through Living Water alone, the movement has enabled more than 350 churches to bless 400,000 people with water and the gospel. God was already at work in the church, planting seeds of discontent with a consumerist Christmas, and a few prophetic pastors devised a creative way to transform that discontent into vibrant worship and positive global change.

Agape Church of Christ

Lest you think such church flourishing is reserved for big churches with charismatic leaders, let's now turn to Agape Church of Christ in Portland, Oregon, where about 75 percent of the church's population was homeless.

I should clarify that Agape is no more. It existed for about ten years before it ceased to meet, but I think you will see its existence and impact as evidence that even in a community with almost no money at all, God can work with passion alone.

For the members of Agape Church, Sunday morning was a chance to come in from the cold, sip hot coffee, and worship in a downtown school while cell phones charged up and down the halls. Agape had its challenges. Someone under the influence of something often interrupted things at the back of the church. Congregants prayed and struggled together through deep issues of God and faith as addiction, illness, or sometimes just plain hard living took their loved ones away. One Sunday when a Living Water representative visited the church, the topic of prayer was a member who had frozen to death the night before. And even there—perhaps *especially* there—God was at work through people's love for one another, as well as for those who had even less than they.

When members of Agape Church heard about Living Water International, they were struck by the fact that, even as poor as they were, they had access to safe drinking water for free at public fountains, yet some did not even have that. They started raising money for the thirsty, mostly by panhandling and working odd jobs.

Over the ten years that Agape Church of Christ existed, they donated more than $30,000 for those in desperate need of safe drinking water.

Liquid Church

Tim Lucas, the founding pastor of Liquid Church in New Jersey, says that Liquid Church "began on accident." Today it is one of America's 100 Fastest Growing Churches with seven campuses spread across the state of New Jersey.[7] Tim has found that those who go on a short-term mission trip return to church on fire about putting their faith into action. He says, "We've found that compassionate cause is a powerful entry point for outsiders, who discover not just a cause to believe in but a God to believe in too."

In his book *Liquid Church: 6 Powerful Currents to Saturate Your City for Christ*[8] Tim describes six currents flowing through our culture that the Holy Spirit is using to reach a new generation for Christ. You will have to buy his book for the other four, but two of my favorite currents are the ones Tim calls "Special Needs" and "Compassionate Cause."

"Special Needs" refers to Liquid Church's efforts to create space at the table for children and adults with autism, Asperger's, and Down syndrome, and lavish God's love on the overlooked. "Compassionate Cause" refers to Liquid Church's mission to bring safe drinking water to the marginalized around the globe, which Tim says "has unleashed an army of compassion, not just in our city, and our state, but around the world."

In 2017, Liquid Church opened its first Clean Water Café. It is staffed by people who have been on a Living Water trip and decorated with enlarged photos from their trips to Central America, Haiti, and Rwanda. The task of Clean Water Café staff is to welcome guests with a cup of hot coffee and raise awareness about Liquid Church's Clean Water

Cause. To welcome new guests, the church makes a $10 donation in the guest's name to people who need safe drinking water. The café was so successful they opened Clean Water Cafés at every campus. The very next year in 2018, they served 66,000 cups of coffee, 5,000 of them to first-time guests.

Figure 11.4. Liquid Church's Clean Water Café

Liquid Church partnered with us to establish the Ruhango WASH Program Area in Rwanda, then to launch another in Busasamana, Rwanda. To date Liquid Church has sponsored over 280 water projects serving more than 100,000 people in nine countries and has sent more than four hundred "Water Warriors" (their name for short-term trip participants) on Living Water trips to El Salvador, Honduras, Guatemala, Haiti, and Rwanda. One recent team of Water Warriors was made up of adults with Down syndrome. The church organized the Central America trip as an esteem-builder to teach participants that God could use them to change the world. They were moved by the fact that these participants were fantastic workers, yet more than 80 percent of Americans with intellectual and developmental disabilities are unemployed. As a result, Liquid Church began to explore an idea for bringing their Special Needs and Compassionate Care programs together.

In 2021, Liquid Church is turning the Clean Water Café at its Broadcast Campus into a full-service coffeehouse that serves breakfast, lunch, and specialty coffee creations. One hundred percent of proceeds will be directed to people in Rwanda who need clean water, better hygiene, and improved sanitation. I love that, of course, but my favorite thing about this new Clean Water Café is that it will be staffed entirely by adults with Asperger's, autism, or Down syndrome from the church's special-needs program.

Bear Creek Community Church and WestGate Church

In Northern California, God was preparing two different churches on two different tracks to join together to increase their impact on the thirsty. In 2007, Bear Creek Community Church in Lodi, California, was seeking a way to make a difference on a global level, but since the country was in a recession, they did not want to ask people for money. They knew they would have to think creatively. Around that time, their children's program director, Ann Pacheco, read that three children die each minute due to water-related illness. She wondered if there was any way the kids of the church could help kids without safe water. She envisioned her kids collecting recyclables by policing their homes, cleaning up their communities and asking others to offer their recyclables to save the lives of thirsty kids around the world. So the children's ministry launched a trial run asking people to bring in their bottles and cans to church. After five months, they looked at the volume of recyclables collected—coupled with California's program to redeem recyclables for a few cents per container—and launched Bear Creek Water as a church-wide initiative.

In 2013, Calvin Breed from WestGate Church in San Jose, California went on a Living Water trip to Guatemala. Calvin met a boy there named Milton whose older sister had died due to lack of safe drinking water. Hearing Milton share his story made the water crisis real for Calvin and his team. After they returned to California, he heard about the recycling program at Bear Creek Community Church. Taking a step of faith, he drove two hours to Lodi to pay them a visit. Together, the two churches not only established a second recycling program at WestGate Church but also started collaborating by sending volunteers to give talks about the world water crisis at churches, business lunches, and schools. They set up recycling collection centers at partner churches, companies, and nonprofits. Members of both churches got their neighbors involved, not only in contributing recyclables, but also going on short-term Living Water trips.

Together, their churches found a way to involve people rich and poor, young and old, Christian and non-Christian alike to change the world. Last I heard, Bear Creek Community Church and WestGate Church had recruited fifteen churches to the Recycle for Water cause, and together they had recycled an estimated 135 tons of plastics and aluminum. With the small amount per container and such a huge volume, they provided safe, sustainable water to more than 100,000 people in 180 communities, schools, and churches around the world.

What I love most about their creative program is the theme of redemption and renewal that runs through it. Together they found a way to redeem trash to bless others and, in the meantime, clean up their own communities and model Christ's unity.

Many more churches are examples of the vitality that grows out of identifying and joining where God is already at work. Pastor Daniel Son knew that was true when he started Church of the Beloved in Renton, Washington. Daniel and his core team asked Living Water International to be a part of their church's DNA from day one. Before they had a building or bought sound equipment or even Bibles, they wrote a check to drill a water well in South Asia. The church has been growing ever since, not in spite of its generosity, but because of it. When Chicago's Christ Community Church and their partners at New Harvest Global Ministries asked Living Water to partner with them in West Africa, we worked together to design our first WASH Program Area in Sierra Leone.

The church set an audacious kickoff fundraising goal of $75,000. Then they overshot that goal, raising not $75,000 but $750,000, funding the WASH Program Area for the next three years!

We may continue to see news about struggling churches in America, but real and lasting change comes from identifying churches that are alive and thriving and then systematically inquiring why. What are the stories that identify the forces and factors that give such life and vitality to each specific community? How can we passionately pursue what enables such a positive impact in people's lives at church, across the street, and around the world? Since God is already at work everywhere, and the opportunities to join him in his saving work are infinite, let us make those stories visible and adaptable wherever we find them—from high-steeple churches to storefronts downtown, in middle-class suburbs, in small towns, or anywhere else. One of the most reliable places to find God at work is where people desire to fulfill God's oldest promise to bless all nations by obeying him.

Churches flourish when they identify and tap into God's design for the church. Next, we will consider some of the key lessons we have learned about inviting these communities, here and abroad, to reflect the one body of Christ.

Reflect

Identify how God is alive and well in your church or in other churches you know.

Write

Record a few exciting ways to make a difference in the world through your church.

Share

Share with your friends what you would like to do through your church to join God in his amazing work of redemption and reconciliation.

SO THAT WE MAY BE ONE

*My prayer is not for them alone. I pray also for those who will believe
in me through their message, that all of them may be one, Father,
just as you are in me and I am in you. May they also be in us
so that the world may believe that you have sent me.*

JOHN 17:20-21

A S WE CONCLUDE our journey of discovery of how God is working throughout his entire body—back in time and across the world—I hope the unity of God and his church has become more visible, attractive, and compelling.

Jesus' final prayer for his followers, before he gave his life for them, was that they would be one (John 17:20-21). The apostle Paul built this image further in Ephesians 4:16 with Jesus as the head of this body holding it together to form a healthy, growing, and mature body of parts that build up the others in love.

Reflection twelve illustrates some unique ways in which the unity of the body of Christ is becoming more visible to us in this twenty-first century while it encourages us to guard that unity.

As I share these stories, I invite you to consider how the unity of the body of Christ is becoming more visible today (or visible in new ways) and how you can celebrate and guard that spiritual reality.

Living Water Trips

I cannot imagine who I would be today if I had not gone on that 1987 trip to Senegal. Gary and Sharon Evans would tell you the same about their 1990 trip to Kenya. Pastor Trey Little would say the same of his first trip to Haiti, as would Greg Holder about his to Zimbabwe. Bishop Horace E. Smith would point to his first visit to Zambia where Princess Zulu showed him around. Most world-changing pastors, ministry leaders, and faithful mission supporters that I know can identify an international trip that connected them to the broader relational network of Christ's body and inspired them to lead widespread, multigenerational change.

Steve Corbett and Brian Fikkert report in their excellent book *When Helping Hurts* that short-term mission trips from the United States exploded from 120,000 in 1989 to 2.2 million in 2006.[1] They also propose ways to appropriately engage across geographical, financial, and cultural dividing lines, pointing out that how we define poverty determines how we engage with others and that different cultures define poverty in different ways. People from wealthy countries often define poverty as a lack of material resources, so they believe its solution is to transfer material resources to the poor. The oppressed tend to define poverty as oppression, so they believe its solution is to work for social justice. Others define poverty in terms of knowledge and see education as its solution. Still others define poverty in terms of personal sin and see evangelization as its solution.

Corbett and Fikkert suggest that a Christian view of poverty should come from a biblical understanding of why Jesus came to earth—to both redeem us and to reconcile all things to God. They build on Bryant L. Myers's important book *Walking with the Poor: Principles and Practices of Transformational Development* in which Myers describes humans as being in relationship with God, self, others, and the rest of creation.[2] If we improve those relationships, we address the poverty Jesus became flesh and blood to address. Equipped by these great thought leaders, members of a mission trip will experience a powerful way to see and guard the unity of the body of Christ.

Living Water has been blessed to host over twenty thousand alumni through its Trips Program—but twenty years ago, this was a vision too big to see. The phenomenon of the short-term mission trip was only just beginning, made possible by the relatively new access to global travel. Upon their return from their first mission trip to Kenya, our cofounders invited their friends and colleagues to join them on the next adventure. The people who crossed those sometimes-scary lines fell in love with those they met there and came back with a new understanding of opportunities to serve and with a passion to make a difference by helping communities access water. To equip them, Living Water started a "drill camp" to teach prospective partners and volunteers the skills they needed to successfully drill a well.

Two drill camp volunteers, Lew and Rita Hough, led the first volunteer trip to Guatemala to facilitate training in the field. Through the Houghs' leadership, a scalable Trips Program developed that hosted volunteers on week-long trips to Guatemala, Honduras, El Salvador, Nicaragua, and Haiti while navigating all the issues around logistics, safety, and the balance between comfort, adventure, authenticity, and liability. Each country operation was made up of high-capacity national leaders and staff who taught visitors to drill wells, install and repair water pumps, and engage the people of the community in basic sanitation and hygiene courses. The visitors bonded with our staff, with community members, and with each other, and thousands of people obtained first-time access to safe water and a fresh view of the body of Christ.

While these trips broadened understanding, built relationships, and demonstrated God's love, our experience and the developing work of thought leaders such as Corbett, Fikkert, and Myers opened our eyes to the possibility that our "helping" may be hurting. Did the model leave the impression on the community that solutions to their problems must come from outside their own community? An unintended consequence was to direct people's attention away from their own material, intellectual, and spiritual resources. Such dynamics reinforce the hosts' sense of powerlessness and inferiority within the body of Christ and deprive the visitors of fully discovering how God was already at work engaging all parts of the body.

This realization led us to reach out to the larger body of believers, which was a true blessing and a source of learning. Drawing on the work of others doing ministry around the world is another way that God's Spirit is weaving our work together. Our Trips Program today includes pretrip and posttrip learning experiences to prepare the traveler to participate in the restoration of relationships—both their own and those of the hosts—to help without hurting and to keep people connected and involved after they return home.

Figure 12.1. Living Water drillers and a Living Water Trip team strike water in a new borehole

As our programs around the world expanded from water provision to WASH Program Areas, and as we started developing long-term relationships to work with and through local churches, we embraced the opportunity for a three-tier Trips Program designed to better serve churches and communities both there and here.

The Learn and Serve Trip introduces participants to the basics of the water crisis as they work alongside local staff with communities for first-time safe water access. Trip activities include water-well drilling, hygiene education, and gospel proclamation, the building blocks of a wider program.

The Connect and Serve Trip teaches participants about implementing WASH activities in the context of long-term community development, including dynamics of church and community mobilization, diverse water solutions, and the challenges of promoting sanitation and hygiene behavior change in communities.

The Sustain and Serve Trip dives even deeper into the community development process. Participants learn how to upgrade an existing water system, participate in program evaluation or capacity assessment activities, and assist in the process of communities transitioning out of Living Water technical and financial support.

All those involved experience a broader and deeper understanding of the body of Christ, each of their roles in it, and the blessing of contributing their gifts to benefit the whole.

Bible Storying Workshops

The apostles never saw the full collection of books we call the Bible or handed out chapters from Gospels according to Matthew, Mark, Luke, or John. For hundreds of years, the gospel of Jesus Christ was spread primarily by stories shared through face-to-face relationships. Yet today an estimated 90 percent of the world's Christian workers present the gospel using highly literate communication styles.[3] That is despite the fact that about 80 percent of people on earth are *oral* communicators who either cannot read or prefer to learn by listening and speaking.[4] In the resource-scarce regions of the world where Living Water International serves, oral-preference learners make up a much higher portion of the population, probably approaching 100 percent. So how can we support people who share the gospel in that context?

President emeritus of Living Water International, Dr. Jerry Wiles, works with the International Orality Network (ION), which highlights that Jesus himself taught by telling stories and asking questions and how the news about Jesus spread the same way.[5] Think of all the Bible's great stories about Jesus—The Woman at the Well, Jesus Calms the Storm, The Triumphal Entry, The Demon-Possessed Gerasene, Nicodemus, The Blind Beggar—all of them convey deeper meaning, and all of them were shared orally.

Those of us who know these stories primarily as written words in Bibles are a minority. Jerry and ION wanted to share what they were learning from oral traditions and to build on this historical, global reality for the spread of God's kingdom. They began what they call Orality, or Bible Storying, to help people in oral cultures share the good news of Jesus Christ through stories and questions. When I joined Living Water, Jerry had already been teaching Bible Storying Workshops around the world for a long time, and to be honest, I was skeptical.

I respected Jerry's passion for helping people share their faith; I just wasn't convinced that this highly educated guy living in Sugar Land, Texas had something to teach people in oral cultures. Then I saw Bible Storying Workshops draw crowds in the United States, Africa, South Asia, Latin America, and the Caribbean. I saw how they provided a forum for convening leaders from diverse churches within a region and helped us reach across the divisions of education, wealth, tribe, and denomination, and focus on commonalities rather than differences. While churches may have their denominational divides and doctrinal disputes, nobody opposes gospel stories about Jesus. All

churches benefit from their members learning to share their faith
through stories and questions.

Consider the story from which Living Water derived its name: Jesus
and the Samaritan woman at the well (from John 4). Most Christians
are generally familiar with this story and you may be tempted to just
skim it and move forward with this book. I invite you to engage with
this story as if you were participating in one of our Bible Storying
Workshops—read every word, memorize the content, and share the
story with a few others who could coach you through the retelling of
this story. The process of learning the story by memory and then re-
peating it draws out its cultural richness and theological depth in new
and sometimes unexpected ways. Try it.

> Now [Jesus] had to go through Samaria. So he came to a town in
> Samaria called Sychar, near the plot of ground Jacob had given
> to his son Joseph. Jacob's well was there, and Jesus, tired as he
> was from the journey, sat down by the well. It was about noon.
>
> When a Samaritan woman came to draw water, Jesus said to
> her, "Will you give me a drink?" (His disciples had gone into the
> town to buy food.)
>
> The Samaritan woman said to him, "You are a Jew and I am
> a Samaritan woman. How can you ask me for a drink?" (For Jews
> do not associate with Samaritans.)
>
> Jesus answered her, "If you knew the gift of God and who it
> is that asks you for a drink, you would have asked him and he
> would have given you living water."
>
> "Sir," the woman said, "you have nothing to draw with and
> the well is deep. Where can you get this living water? Are you
> greater than our father Jacob, who gave us the well and drank
> from it himself, as did also his sons and his livestock?"
>
> Jesus answered, "Everyone who drinks this water will be
> thirsty again, but whoever drinks the water I give them will

never thirst. Indeed, the water I give them will become in them
a spring of water welling up to eternal life."

The woman said to him, "Sir, give me this water so that I won't
get thirsty and have to keep coming here to draw water."

He told her, "Go, call your husband and come back."

"I have no husband," she replied.

Jesus said to her, "You are right when you say you have no
husband. The fact is, you have had five husbands, and the man
you now have is not your husband. What you have just said is
quite true."

"Sir," the woman said, "I can see that you are a prophet. Our
ancestors worshiped on this mountain, but you Jews claim that
the place where we must worship is in Jerusalem."

"Woman," Jesus replied, "believe me, a time is coming when
you will worship the Father neither on this mountain nor in
Jerusalem. You Samaritans worship what you do not know; we
worship what we do know, for salvation is from the Jews. Yet a
time is coming and has now come when the true worshipers will
worship the Father in the Spirit and in truth, for they are the
kind of worshipers the Father seeks. God is spirit, and his worshipers must worship in the Spirit and in truth."

The woman said, "I know that Messiah" (called Christ) "is
coming. When he comes, he will explain everything to us."

Then Jesus declared, "I, the one speaking to you—I am he."
(John 4:4-26)

While sitting under a tree in the middle of nowhere, I have joined
conversations about religion, racism, ethnic and tribal conflict,
worship, physical and spiritual thirst, and water and living water,
flowing from that story alone.

People in oral cultures usually learn and retell these Bible stories
with more ease and less self-consciousness than people in highly

literate, print-based cultures. We regularly receive reports like this letter from Pastor Cornel in Kenya:

> Thank you so much for extending your invitation to our secretary Brigid Akoth to attend the Bible Storying Workshop in Kisumu. . . . As the pastor of Milimani Baptist Church, I have begun to see the fruits of the seminar. . . . I have to confess it was the first time we taught a Bible study through storytelling. We were all seated in a circle as Brigid accurately narrated the story of the Samaritan Woman at the Well. To my amazement, by the time she finished more than half the church could accurately tell the story! My confession is that we have never had a very powerful tool like this in our church. . . . You have also permanently impacted Brigid's life. . . . May God continue to richly reward you. Please if you get more opportunity for training, we kindly beg you to consider us.

Pastor Cornel went on to share that Brigid's enthusiasm has led her husband, George, to Christ, for which Brigid and Pastor Cornel had been praying for many years. Since then, Brigid has facilitated workshops at a number of churches in eastern Kenya and in the Kisumu women's prison.

Or there is the story of Matilda Tarr, whose broken home forced her to work as a peanut vendor at the age of seven. Older boys and men often took advantage of street kids like Matilda, who was a mother of two by the age of fourteen. Then Liberia's civil war tore her family apart too. Her daughter went missing. Matilda was captured, made a prisoner of war, rescued by a Nigerian peacekeeper, then lived as a refugee in Sierra Leone, then in Nigeria, where an older woman led her to Christ. Matilda got married, earned a degree in Christian counseling, then started rescuing young girls and taking them into her home. She started an organization called "Destiny Women International" to help girls become the women God destined them to be. With money she saved from counseling jobs, she bought airtime for a radio program called "The Hour of Destiny!" What could we possibly teach a firecracker like Matilda about sharing the gospel?

She put it this way:

> My church sent me to Ghana to be trained in sharing the gospel through stories. When I came home it was like fire! I trained women at my church. To women who can't read or write, I said—no matter! You can preach! You can teach! You can tell gospel stories. You can be a Woman of Destiny!

Visit Matilda today and you might find her among her Women of Destiny, an army of saints who hit the streets with interlocked arms, addressing one another's needs and cultivating disciples of Christ.

The power of stories and questions is that they often spread in ways that paper and ink don't. When Zimbabwean evangelist Davis Mambure shared the story of Jesus and the Blind Beggar in the rural Murehwa district, he could never have imagined where the conversations he started would lead. The topic of the beggar's blindness, which includes a rebuke from the leaders for calling out to Jesus, quickly led to conversations about barriers that prohibit victims of torture and abuse from being heard in Murehwa district today. Participants acknowledged that there was a culture of silence and shame around certain issues in their lives, then started talking about the number of twelve- and thirteen-year-old girls in their communities who were forced to marry, which led to what they considered to be legally sanctioned child sexual abuse.

Davis Mambure's report on the workshop touched the heart of Reverend Lindani Dube, the Evangelical Fellowship of Zimbabwe's general secretary. When he was invited to participate in Zimbabwe's celebration of the Day of the African Child, Rev. Dube raised the issue discussed in the Murehwa Bible Storying Workshop and challenged policy makers to ban child marriages. Government authorities in attendance made a commitment to look into this matter of child marriages. With Christian voices added to others challenging this practice, Zimbabwe's constitutional court passed a law banning marriages of any person below eighteen years of age.

Witnessing how the Holy Spirit is moving among listeners of oral Bible stories—many of whom are willing to cross dividing lines to learn about Jesus' life—is exciting and so inspiring! As we engaged in the global body of Christ, Living Water International adopted a new way to communicate biblical truths using the most appropriate methodology for oral learners. Moreover, the common language of both storyteller and listener facilitates an understanding of biblical truths that transcend divides.

The Genius of One

You might recall that when Living Water International and Pastor Greg Holder's church, The Crossing, partnered with the Evangelical Fellowship of Zimbabwe, they understood this partnership to be a direct answer to their prayers.

You may also recall from reflection ten how EFZ was an answer to Living Water's prayers as EFZ's Humanitarian Relief and Development Commission worked with our regional vice president for Africa to develop the program they called Salt and Light. This offered an extraordinary education for us. It informed our decision to expand our work from water interventions alone to full WASH: water access, sanitation, and hygiene. It informed our commitment to work with and through local churches to save lives, cultivate fully formed disciples of Jesus Christ, and do our part to fulfill Jesus' prayer that his followers would be one. The relationships that developed as we worked together enabled us all to accomplish so much more than we could independently. The story is bigger yet!

As a result of The Crossing's passion to act on God's call to bless and serve the church and EFZ's passion to be salt and light, Living Water gathered about 250 local church leaders in Zimbabwe's capital city, Harare, for a church capacity building conference. I couldn't blame the local pastors for looking skeptical as they sat back in their chairs with arms crossed. I would be skeptical too if I were a Zimbabwean whose country had a long history of clashes between Blacks and Whites over property rights and other tribal conflict. I would probably be sitting back in my chair with arms folded too, looking at the pastors from Missouri and thinking, *What could these* wazungu *possibly have to teach me?*

Then Greg spoke about unity among believers, the power of forgiveness, the poison of gossip, and other compelling biblical truths, and arms unfolded. People leaned forward. A spirit of unity was unleashed in the room, and it felt miraculous. Pastors told us that the messages and the practical application of biblical principles was *exactly* what the church in Zimbabwe needed, and they wanted more.

Attendance at these kinds of events normally drops day by day. People show up to honor their relationship with the host, then attendance dwindles after they have met their obligation. Yet for us it was the opposite. After day one, attendees called their friends and invited them to join us on day two. Requests to accommodate new guests poured in, and Living Water's local staff raced to adjust logistics, food, and water as attendance leaped from 250 to 400, and once again it happened: arms unfolded, people leaned forward, a spirit of unity was unleashed. Debriefing with Greg and his team from The Crossing afterward, we all wondered at what we had just witnessed. Certain that we had seen the Holy Spirit at work, we decided to do a similar conference the following year. Was it just this time and place or was the Spirit at work elsewhere?

The following year, the three partners organized a conference three hundred miles away from Harare in Bulawayo. We did not know it at the time, but EFZ was balancing longstanding ethnic rivalries between Harare's Shona people and Bulawayo's Ndebele people so one tribe would not feel favored by EFZ over the other. We refined our content and presentation alongside the local church facilitators. It was the same routine once again: Arms unfolded. People leaned forward. A spirit of unity was unleashed. Attendance grew from day one to day two. Everyone said this was *exactly* what they needed, and they wanted more.

Now we wondered whether the Holy Spirit was at work in the same way in different cultural and religious contexts. The following year we set our sights on Sierra Leone, where the population is nearly 80 percent Muslim. We asked the Evangelical Fellowship of Sierra Leone to coordinate the conference. Once again, we refined our content and our presentation. Once again church leaders started out skeptical, then arms unfolded. People leaned forward. A spirit of unity was unleashed. Attendance grew from day one to day two. Everyone said this was *exactly* what they needed, and they wanted more.

It bothered us that so many people missed the important first day of the conference. Our next conference would be in Zambia, so in hopes to improve first-day attendance at subsequent conferences, we invited the presidents and general directors of the Evangelical Fellowship in each of the nine African countries where we work. Word spread, and in Zambia more participants attended from the beginning, but we also received delegations from countries where Living Water did not work. With these key leaders in attendance, the national conference became a continental event that attracted the attention of news media and elected officials.

The day after the Zambia conference, The Crossing and Living Water debriefed with dignitaries from across the continent, and they too said this message was *exactly* what churches in their countries needed. The Reverend Dr. Goodwill Shana, president of the Association of Evangelicals in Africa, gave the conference his blessing and sparked interest from the Evangelical Fellowships across the continent to explore partnerships with us.

Over the years as the conference schedule grew, Greg wrote a book about God's answer for our fractured world called *The Genius of One.*[6] We decided that Genius of One was the perfect name for our conference, so we started calling it that and gave out Greg's book to equip the pastors with a resource to utilize within their own networks.

Now we were kind of getting addicted! If the Holy Spirit was wanting to expand the bench and broaden the network, we'd get ready. *Swing us again!* The Crossing and Living Water took The Genius of One Conference *on tour* in East Africa with evangelical fellowships in Uganda, Kenya, and Rwanda. We involved all our regional staff and invited the African leaders we worked with, board members, and other pastors from the West. We spread the word to other Christian NGOs and whoever else we thought would be interested in the idea.

The president of Hope International, Peter Greer, showed up to the final conference in Rwanda. His visionary book *Rooting for Rivals* reflected the same message we saw emerging in conferences across

Figure 12.2. The Genius of One Conference in Kigali, Rwanda, in 2019

Africa—better together, even when it's hard! We started dreaming of how Hope International's microcredit program might work with our WASH program. We began to identify other complementary, values-aligned ministries that might consider working together as one.

Uganda was our first stop, and President Yoweri Museveni not only showed up, but he preached! Museveni has been President of Uganda for nearly thirty-five years, many of them challenged by regional conflict. Not everyone in attendance was convinced of the strong leader's Christian witness, but nobody could doubt that he knew his way around the Bible, both Old and New Testaments. He could preach, and he was gracious in recognizing the Christ-centeredness of Living Water International.

"My wife has been telling me about Living Water International for years," President Museveni said, "and it is clear that you follow Jesus Christ. You never talk about yourselves publicly, but I have been watching you and it is clear to me that following Jesus Christ is at the center of your work. I will be selling some of my cows to support the work of Living Water International!"

A presidential endorsement can go a long way in terms of opening doors for the church as a serious partner in community life. Serving as the body of Christ continues to include many stakeholders across the dividing lines of politics and economics in Uganda. Whether the president decided to join the conference for political, humanitarian, or relational purposes, his public affirmation of the role and work of the church was a door opener for us and highlighted the important role that the national church, alongside churches at the district and local level, could play in relaying the message of unity and touching lives for Christ.

The role of the church in international development through Christian ministries like ours is also gaining prominence on the global stage. "We're past the question of whether or why development organizations should engage with local faith actors," Katherine Marshall told a group of international NGO leaders assembled at a recent World Bank roundtable. "Today, the question is how."[7]

Marshall, a senior fellow at Georgetown University's Berkley Center for Religion, Peace & World Affairs, leads the center's work on religion and global development. She worked at the World Bank for thirty-five years and has studied development issues facing the world's poorest countries. She sees a large and growing role for churches in international development. More specifically, she sees communities of faith playing a special role in WASH programs.

As she pointed out in a 2013 policy brief,

> Water is also an integral part of rituals and the beliefs and teachings of virtually every major world religion and spiritual tradition. Faith leaders and institutions are active on water issues.
> ... They have the potential to play far larger roles than they now do in advancing water and sanitation advocacy and programs.

Though the Uganda conference was my first personal interaction with Uganda's president, we had been working with Uganda's First Lady Janet Museveni, fondly known as "Mama Janet," for a decade. She invited us to the statehouse the day after the conference and we relived our personal stories of all the challenges and blessings of working together to access water and share the good news of Jesus with approximately forty thousand people throughout the Western Ugandan Ntungamo district. Tears rolled down her face as she related what a blessing it has been to see Jesus live through his people and his church. She mentioned that she had been telling her husband about our work all these years.

"It seems you have," I said. "He sounded like he was a bishop yesterday—he was *preaching*!"

Mama Janet chuckled and said, "A bishop? Not quite yet."

"And," I could not resist, "he said he's going to sell some cows to bless even more people in Uganda."

"Oh, he is?"

"Yes," I said as I kept smiling and invited her to Houston, "maybe you could use that cow money to come to our gala in October? You could sponsor a really big table." Mama Janet kept smiling as she diverted our attention by suggesting that we take some photographs together. In one she's holding my arm and Natalie's hand, glowing from our time together reminiscing. As everyone left, Mama Janet held me back so I would be last to leave.

"I can't make it to that gala," she said, with a handshake saying goodbye, "but we'll be sending you a $100,000 gift on behalf of the people of Uganda."

God continues his work in Uganda!

From Uganda, our tour took us to Kenya, then Rwanda, and everywhere we went, The Genius of One Conference continued to foster unity—from the biblically-based content presented, to the relational experience of the events, to the partnerships formed at them. As a result, we started signing formal cooperation agreements with the various Evangelical Fellowship organizations in the countries where we worked. We formalized relationships with other nongovernmental organizations and government ministries. We gained the favor of key political figures and experienced a geometric expansion of relationships that informed the way we approached WASH; we made long-term commitments to WASH Program Areas; and we launched the church mobilization toolset we call Flourish. Once again, the Master Strategist was at work on a vision too big for us to see.

After our East Africa tour, we once again debriefed to discern where the Holy Spirit would bring us next. There was no longer any doubt that the Spirit was on the move, and we wanted to dive deeper. We started thinking of everyone we could invite into the trans-Africa tour, in terms of our African partners and church leaders as well as North American church leaders that would be excited about jumping in. What about Latin America and the Caribbean? South Asia? The United States?

So That You May Be ONE

Pastor Greg snaps fingers at one second intervals to illustrate the pressure of time while he shares a story about the night Jesus was betrayed. Jesus was in his dark night of the soul and the clock was ticking, *snap, snap, snap*, when he prayed. Jesus prayed for himself, then for his disciples, then for all who would ever believe in him—us. He did not pray that we would all be brave, or that we would all be relevant. He prayed that we would all "be one, Father, just as you are in me and I am in you" (see John 17:21).

In part three of this book, I have shared with you a handful of stories from the dozens I have observed in my journeys around the world. God's vision is truly too big to see, but we are given glimpses. God invites us to join him as he is already at work through his church over there, is moving through his church here, and continues to build and make visible the one body of Christ back in time and around the world.

Our friends from Zimbabwean churches taught us about how God is already at work in Africa and how to mobilize and empower churches for WASH-focused community development. Those lessons informed our strategic plans, the evolution of our programs from water to WASH, the way we work within WASH Program Areas, and our approach to church mobilization and community development.

Our friends from Latin American and Caribbean churches taught us that God is already at work in Latin America and gave us language for the "integral mission of the church" as the inseparable proclamation and demonstration of the gospel, seen in the life and works of Jesus Christ. These ideas informed our Theory of Change, the Flourish toolkit, and our philosophy and approach to gospel proclamation globally.

Our friends from South Asian churches taught us that God is already at work in Asia and that we are engaged in a spiritual battle. From them we learned how to pray when in the face of crisis and how to organize ourselves around spiritual disciplines, making time and space for prayer and incorporating it into everything we do.

Figure 12.3. Jesus prayed that we would all be one, just as he and the father are one

Our friends from American churches have taught us that God is moving through the church in America. As those churches engage in their own communities, throughout their cities, and with friends around the world, they offer insights on how we can better serve with the church as it cultivates disciples at home and to the ends of the earth.

These are just a few of the stories that illustrate how the Holy Spirit has been weaving various threads into a tapestry to fulfill Jesus' prayer that we may all be one. We have been served while at the same time serving others. God's glory is reflected in the whole while each strand, taken from seemingly unrelated areas, is being woven by the Master Strategist to redeem and reconcile the world.

I am curious to see the full extent of how the coronavirus pandemic impacts God's redemption story. We have already seen that the relationships built among church networks remain alive and actively engaged in global prayer. Church relationships built while we were able to gather and travel, in combination with technology, have enabled us to facilitate Covid-19 prevention messages and WASH resources to help churches fight the virus. Bible Storying Workshops have been modified for smaller groups of participants to accommodate social distancing. We are exploring new, virtual ways of relating across dividing lines as we eagerly await a return to international travel. How is the Holy Spirit moving among us during the pandemic to unite us to serve God and reflect his glory?

These stories offer tremendous comfort and hope as we face a global pandemic that has once again changed everything. The day coronavirus concerns canceled all international flights in the spring of 2020, Living Water International took a revenue hit of nearly 20 percent. Across the globe, livelihoods were negatively affected. Each of our operational leaders in eighteen countries scrambled to understand the virus and position their teams to continue to equip the church to fight Covid-19. In these contexts, social distancing, quarantining, and handwashing are difficult to achieve because so many people share small homes, survive through day labor, and lack access to water and soap. Water, sanitation, and hygiene are three keys to physical health in this pandemic, just as they have been in the past and will be in pandemics to come. The living water Jesus offers is the key to spiritual health in this crisis, just as it was in the past and will be in crises to come.

During this global crisis, although I struggle daily about how to proceed in uncertain times, I stand firm on the knowledge and experience that God has equipped his church—and Living Water International as a partner to the church—to carry on his mission. I do not know how the pandemic will end, or if it will end, but I do know that God has not been blindsided and continues to invite us to serve him through his church for a vision too big for me to see.

Even as the coronavirus pandemic has forced us into social isolation, it has opened our eyes to see how God has been forming us into one interconnected, global body of Christ. We recognize that as one body, we have been being prepared for days when we would not be able to physically go or gather but still long to continue God's work. Thanks to the internet and our church networks on the ground, within six months of the onset of the pandemic we were able to implement custom-made coronavirus responses supporting 7,000 churches, hosting 1,500 hygiene and sanitation workshops, and equipping 600 healthcare facilities. The technology also provided a platform for continued collective prayer.

Never before has the church possessed the resources we now have for repairing relationships with God, self, others, and the rest of creation at a global scale. Affordable, fast international travel equipped us to foster relationships between individuals, communities, and churches. Shared language and translation technology enable us to continue to pray, dream, and plan together. The internet, smartphones, apps, and personal computers connect us instantly as we video conference, upload and download real-time reports anywhere in the world, and worship together across the lines that divide us.

Think about how the biggest shifts in human history are driven by changes in travel and communication technology. The famous *viae Romanae,* or Roman roads, were a quarter million miles of government-constructed roads, fifty thousand miles of them paved. This infrastructure, combined with religious persecution, contributed to the spread of early Christianity as missionaries dispersed, sharing their message. To a significant degree, we owe the New Testament's availability to a print innovation called the *codex* in Rome at the time of Christ. The predecessor to the modern book, a codex is a stack of papyrus pages bound at one end. It was a more convenient, less expensive print technology that would eventually replace the scroll. All the earliest New Testament manuscripts are in codex form, as are all the earliest lectionaries, letters, and songbooks of early Christianity.

Perhaps the most famous example of communication technology affecting Christian culture is the role of the printing press in the Protestant Reformation. New forms of communication such as flyers and pamphlets made new ideas, thoughts, and doctrine available to the public in ways that had never been seen before. Household Bibles in native tongues transformed Christian faith throughout Europe, and the world has not been the same ever since.

Today we are in the midst of a travel and communication technology revolution that will outstrip both the codex and the printing press by comparison. The internet, computer, smartphone, and related technologies, pressured by a worldwide pandemic, are already ushering in a new world. A question for us is what role the body of Christ will have in programming and utilizing them. How will we tell the stories of God's faithfulness through his church? Will we actively use our new technologies to steer our story in the direction God wants for us and the world?

God is *always* inviting his church to join him as he rescues and reconciles the world. The most exciting thing about these twenty-first-century tools is that they offer us an opportunity to participate in what the Master Strategist has always been planning for the end of our story together, a vision wherein we see ourselves, members of one body, united with Christ, and behold!

Reflect

Recall what you have seen, heard, or experienced related to the oneness of Christ's body in your church at home, across your city, or around the world.

Write

List new opportunities, large or small, to reflect and protect the unity of Christ's body.

Share

Share with someone you trust a step or two that you will take to celebrate and guard that unity.

BEHOLD, THE MASTER STRATEGIST

An Invitation to Share Your Stories

Behold, I make all things new.

REVELATION 21:5 (KJV)

I AM GRATEFUL for the dark night of the soul that dropped me to my knees and invited me (and then us) to journey back through time and around the world to rediscover God's gifts of the Bible, love, faith, hope, family, community, city, and world; to recall how God's vision in each of our lives is too big for us to see in the moment but that he is active in our lives and through his body—the church—redeeming and reconciling this world.

The way we humans make sense of things is by telling stories. Through stories, God reveals himself to us in Scripture, and by telling stories, we discover what gives us life. We tell stories to craft a shared vision of our future together. Our stories unite us and compel us to take action. As we submit that action to the story being told by a Master Strategist who knows us, loves us, and invites us into his divine plan, we find our roles in the greatest story ever told.

As you read this epilogue, I invite you to recall stories of God at work in your own life and that of your church—stories you could share to help others better understand, celebrate, and replicate God's work of redemption and reconciliation in our world.

⸗⸗⸗⸗⸗⸗⸗⸗⸗⸗⸗

My father had just died, Natalie had cancer, we were in an economic recession, fundraising was flopping, then oil prices tanked. Relationships were stressed at work, Hurricane Harvey devastated our city, and half our board said we should cancel our annual gala. Feeling spiritually alone one sleepless night, I opened my Bible to the verse that framed our gala theme, "To the Ends of the Earth."

I could relate to the disciples. Their faith must have hit rock bottom before Jesus appeared to them and told them they would be his witnesses "in Jerusalem, and in all Judea and Samaria, and to the ends of the earth" (Acts 1:8). I certainly felt like I was at rock bottom that early morning. Then, after months of silence, I finally heard God speak.

I drove to work, gathered our communications team, and told them I had an idea that I believed was divinely inspired. I shared that I thought God had told me to ask our neighbors in "Judea and Samaria" to "stand in the gap" for Houston after the hurricane, so we could continue to be a blessing to the ends of the earth.

Filming from the flooded home of one of our employees, we shot a video telling the world that the people of Houston could not respond to the thirsty this year, and we needed others to stand in the gap to help us raise the $1.8 million anticipated deficit caused by Hurricane Harvey. Confident our plan was from the Lord, we launched a three-week "Stand in the Gap" campaign by internet, email, and social media. By the end of week one we had raised $46,000, which was great . . . but it wasn't $1.8 million.

We gathered, prayed, and decided our second week's strategy would be just to call everyone we knew and ask them to participate. I asked my friends Joe and Hollis Bullard to give their $50,000 pledge early to help show some progress on our website's fundraising thermometer. Natalie called her mom who had an IRA distribution she gave to charity each year, and she sent $10,000 our way. We called pastors, old friends, and people from Chicago. We tweeted, emailed, and posted our video on Facebook and Instagram; by the end of week two we had $110,000, which was great . . . but it wasn't $1.8 million.

With one week to go, I stared at the fundraising thermometer on our website, which showed 6 percent progress toward our goal. I felt vulnerable and started to doubt that "Stand in the Gap" really came from God. I'm not proud of how cranky I felt as I drove out to visit Living Water cofounder and friend Gary Loveless. I knew he didn't have the resources we needed available at the moment, but I always enjoyed visiting him. As I drove to his office, I prayed out loud in the car and, though I'm embarrassed to share this, I started complaining to God by naming people out loud who I knew had the resources to help but had not responded to my emails and calls.

"How you doing?" Gary welcomed me into his office.

"Gary, I've never before said this to you, but I am discouraged. Living Water is going to run out of cash and I'm afraid that I'm steering this ship onto the rocks. We're about to max out our line of credit, and I don't know how we're going to replace that money. I called six people who I know could help, and not one has responded. People are stressed out. I'm stressed out, Gary . . . I'm not doing well."

Gary, seemingly unmoved, did not react but rather smiled and inquired, "How's Natalie?"

"She's fine."

"And the kids?"

"Oh, they're fine, Gary, thanks," I said, warming as I reordered my priorities.

"Well, I've been praying about this 'Stand in the Gap' thing, and I've been talking about it to some friends, and I hope this will help." Gary slid a handwritten check across the table and said, "I think it's $100,000," then he paused, "I might've miscounted the zeros."

As I studied the check I was now holding, I realized it was a hand-written check for $1,000,000 signed by someone with whom I was not yet familiar, who had never given us a gift of any size and was completely invisible to us. Through a longtime friendship with Gary, this couple was introduced to Living Water and had decided to stand in the gap with us. The Lord continued to reveal his faithfulness as I drove home—all six of the people that I'd "called out" in my prayer just a few hours before had reached out to me while I was with Gary. Not all of them could give, but they all responded. Overcome with immense gratitude for God's undeniable presence in my discouragement, I pulled my car over to acknowledge his faithfulness and ask forgiveness for my lack of faith and for my very human complaining.

Two days before the gala as we were rehearsing, a pastor friend texted, "I have three questions. Call me." I called and answered his questions, then as an afterthought he added, "Oh, by the way, we moved some property around and we're going to wire you $460,000 . . . I wanted you to know that before the gala."

Overwhelmed by the gift, I walked into the room where our marketing team watched us rehearse and cried, "Dial up that thermometer! We have another $460,000!"

"This is crazy!" someone shouted, and I noticed our gala cochairs leave the room.

"Dial it up another $200,000!" they exclaimed upon return. Then our vice president of development told me I needed to rewrite my "Stand in the Gap" speech.

Incredulous, I asked, "What do you mean? The gala's in just two days!"

"Mike," he said with tears in his eyes, "The Lord has already stood in the gap . . . now we need to ask people to go with us *to the ends of the earth!*"

By the day of our gala, God had answered our prayers with exactly the $1.8 million we needed to keep going, all of it from sources that had been invisible to us before our divinely inspired "Stand in the Gap" campaign, reminding us that God is indeed the Master Strategist.

Several months prior to all this, Natalie had completed radiation treatment and had rung the bell at Houston Methodist Sugar Land Hospital to declare her victory over cancer. She stood like a triumphant prizefighter looking over her shoulder at God in her corner. To this day that bell reminds me how sweet life is, how wonderful memories are, and how precious love is. God does not always extend our time on earth when we ask for it. Natalie and I have lost some dearly loved ones along the way. Perhaps you have too, and if you're like me, it is deeply reassuring to know how the story ends and how each of our stories are woven into the story God is telling through all of creation.

Figure 13.1. Natalie ringing the bell at the conclusion of radiation treatments

Perhaps the most powerful and fulfilling example of how the tributaries of our life stories flow together into the river of life is the story of water, a story of God's love, as traced through the Bible.

"In the beginning" at the start of Genesis, God hovered over water before separating it into the waters above and those below (Genesis 1:1). This all happened in Eden where "streams came up from the earth and watered the whole surface of the ground," then gathered into a river "watering the garden," which "flowed from Eden" (Genesis 2:6, 10). We can follow that imagery of water reflecting God's love throughout the Bible from the headwaters of Eden to the sea Moses parted; to water springing forth from a rock; to the Jordan River Joshua crossed into the Promised Land—the Jordan Elisha used to heal his enemy Naaman; the Jordan of John's baptism, Jesus' baptism, and the waters of your baptism too—to the water Jesus turns to wine in Cana; to Jesus offering the Samaritan woman "living water"; to the water that pours forth from Jesus' heart after he dies on the cross. In fact, those water images flow all the way to Scripture's final scene, which circles back to the water of life, concluding in Revelation:

> Then I saw "a new heaven and a new earth," for the first heaven and the first earth had passed away. . . . I saw the Holy City, the new Jerusalem, coming down out of heaven from God, prepared as a bride beautifully dressed for her husband. (Revelation 21:1-2)

The story that began with an image of God's quintessential creation, the Garden of Eden, ends with an image of humankind's quintessential creation: the city, in its perfection as the Holy City, the bride of Christ, the church—us—one with a God who rules all creation, declaring from his throne, "Behold, I make all things new" (Revelation 21:5 KJV)!

"Then the angel showed me the river of the water of life," the Bible's final chapter begins, "as clear as crystal, flowing from the throne of God" (Revelation 22:1). The chapter then describes the bountiful tree of life on the shores of that river, its leaves for the healing of the nations. God's pursuit of our love is complete in this scene; the Spirit of God and his bride are together at last, extending this invitation as one:

> The Spirit and the bride say, "Come!" And let the one who hears say, "Come!" Let the one who is thirsty come; and let the one who wishes take the free gift of the water of life. (Revelation 22:17)

As God's Holy Spirit empowers and guides us, our every action becomes a thread God is weaving into the tapestry that reveals this final scene, an image of God and humankind as one, offering the free gift of the water of life. It is a vision we can participate in this very day as we offer life to sisters and brothers near and far, and even to the ends of the earth.

Join the conversation—what's your story? If we can use technology to track the spread of a virus from person to person, boarding planes, crossing seas, and moving through our cities, could we not use that same technology to track the spread of God's love across our relationships and throughout the world?

Stories of love, faith, hope, family, community, city, and world soothe our souls, deepen and enrich our relationships, and bring to light the truth that we are always loved and never alone. The almighty and all-knowing God longs to know us and continues to invite us into relationship with him and with each other—to the ends of the earth! Our stories reflect and reinforce this truth. Tell your story!

Reflect

Reread your own story notes from the twelve reflections in this book.

Write

Draft your story using one or more of your reflections.

Share

Share that story with someone you trust.

I invite you to record your story in written, audio, or video form, and submit it online at https://thirstingforlivingwater.com/stories, where you will see others' stories too.

ACKNOWLEDGMENTS

WRITING A BOOK, like building a house, earning a degree, or raising a family, is best done as a team. As with life's other great journeys, we may never have begun this one had we comprehended its challenges, but then again, we would never have experienced its tremendous blessings.

My friend Paul Dařílek suggested to Natalie and me four years ago that I write a book. The three of us had collaborated frequently on my speeches and video scripts and each of us had written articles, book chapters, and dissertations, but none of us had completed a book.

We equipped ourselves with a whiteboard, the internet, legal pads, and a tape recorder. We read books on how to craft a book proposal and talked to author friends, who introduced us to their agents and publishers and helped us refine our thinking. We clarified the audience, crafted an initial framework, and selected stories to tell. We researched, we fact-checked, we theologized. We went round and round for months, negotiating the approach, language, story arc, framework, chapter headings, titles, Bible verses, and every other aspect of the emerging book. As months became years, our individual contributions blended into a collective whole.

By Christmas 2020, we had a rough draft to send to our focus group—the thirty people whose stories you have encountered in *Thirsting for Living Water*. Each of them responded with their encouragement, suggestions, edits, permissions, and approvals. Many of them offered significant constructive input, some of them read every word, and a few of them became coeditors with us, including Jim Ludema, Gordon Murphy, Cal Jen, Corey Mantel and other family members, our daughters, and their significant others. We are so grateful to everyone who participated in this effort. Engaging with our dear family and friends was deeply moving as we relived the joy and pain of our shared life and were filled with an overwhelming sense of God's faithfulness through it all.

Our team grew to include the marketing and communications team at Living Water, who collected photos, crafted illustrations, and further refined our language. Amber Johnson along with the Wilks Communications Group joined us to coordinate our shared marketing efforts and to get us over the finish line. We are grateful to the skilled editors at InterVarsity Press, Ethan McCarthy and Emily Varner, along with their exceptional administrative and marketing teams for their experience and guidance.

We hope that this shared effort will encourage others to recall their own stories of God's faithfulness and to embark on a journey with their friends to share them and change the world. Thank you one and all!

NOTES

Introduction

[1]Saint John of the Cross, *Dark Night of the Soul And Other Great Works* (Alachua, FL: Bridge Logos Foundation, 2007).

Reflection 2. Love Is a Spiritual Practice

[1]"Cancer Statistics," Understanding Cancer, National Cancer Institute of the National Institute of Health, updated September 25, 2020, www.cancer.gov/about-cancer/understanding/statistics.

Reflection 3. Your Faith Will Be Tested

[1]"About Living Water," Living Water International, https://water.cc/about livingwater/.

[2]Kevin Watkins et al., *Human Development Report 2006: Beyond Scarcity: Power, Poverty, and the Global Water Crisis* (New York: United Nations Development Programme, 2006), 45.

[3]"Diarrhoeal Disease," Fact Sheets, World Health Organization, May 2, 2017, www.who.int/en/news-room/fact-sheets/detail/diarrhoeal-disease.

[4]Watkins, *Human Development Report 2006*, 6, 8.

[5]Guy Hulton, *Global Costs and Benefits of Drinking-Water Supply and Sanitation Interventions to Reach the MDG Target and Universal Coverage*, WHO/HSE/WSH/12.01 (Geneva, Switzerland: World Health Organization, 2012), 4.

[6]"The Right to Water," Fact Sheet No. 35, United Nations Office of the High Commissioner for Human Rights (OHCHR), (New York: United Nations, 2010), 10.

[7]UNICEF, "UNICEF: Collecting Water Is Often a Colossal Waste of Time for Women and Girls," August 29, 2016, www.unicef.org/press-releases/unicef-collecting-water-often-colossal-waste-time-women-and-girls.

[8]D. L. Cooperrider and S. Srivastva, "Appreciative Inquiry in Organizational Life," in *Research in Organizational Change and Development*, vol. 1, ed. W. A. Pasmore and R. W. Woodman (Greenwich, CT: JAI Press, 1987), 129-69; J. D. Ludema et al., *The Appreciative Inquiry Summit: A Practitioner's Guide for Leading Large-Scale Change* (San Francisco:

Berrett-Koehler Publishers, 2003); J. D. Ludema, M. R. Manning, and A. A. Johnson, *Six Questions That Can Lift Your Leadership, Shape Your Strategy, and Transform Your Organization* (Lisle, IL: Center for Values-Driven Leadership, Benedictine University, 2016), https://cvdl.ben.edu/resources-tools/six-questions/.

Reflection 4. Wait for the Gift Promised by the Father

[1]John D. Murphy, National Weather Service, Service Assessment: *August–September 2017 Hurricane Harvey* (Silver Spring, Maryland: US Department of Commerce, National Oceanic and Atmospheric Administration, and National Weather Service, 2018), www.weather.gov/media/publications/assessments/harvey6-18.pdf.

[2]Bill Chappell, "National Weather Service Adds New Colors So It Can Map Harvey's Rains," *The Two Way* (blog). *NPR*, August 28, 2017, www.npr.org/sections/thetwo-way/2017/08/28/546776542/national-weather-service-adds-new-colors-so-it-can-map-harveys- rains.

[3]David M. Roth, "Tropical Cyclone Point Maxima," *Tropical Cyclone Rainfall Data*, United States Weather Prediction Center, accessed March 19, 2021, www.wpc.ncep.noaa.gov/tropical/rain/tcmaxima.html.

[4]Mark Fischetti, "Hurricane Harvey: Why Is It So Extreme?" *Scientific American* 28 (August 28, 2017).

[5]Fischetti, "Hurricane Harvey"; Eric S. Blake and David A. Zelinsky, *National Hurricane Center Tropical Cyclone Report: Hurricane Harvey*, National Hurricane Center, National Oceanographic and Atmospheric Administration, AL092017 (2018).

[6]Angela Fritz and Jason Samenow, "Harvey Unloaded 33 Trillion Gallons of Water in the US," *Capital Weather Gang* (blog), *The Washington Post*, September 27, 2017, www.washingtonpost.com/news/capital-weather-gang/wp/2017/08/30/harvey-has-unloaded-24-5-trillion-gallons-of-water-on-texas-and-louisiana/.

[7]Jason Samenow, "Harvey Is a 1,000-Year Flood Event Unprecedented in Scale," *Capital Weather Gang* (blog), *Washington Post*, August 31, 2017, www.washingtonpost.com/news/capital-weather-gang/wp/2017/08/31/harvey-is-a-1000-year-flood-event-unprecedented-in-scale/.

[8]*CBS Sunday Morning*, "Harvey: A Disaster of Biblical Proportions," aired September 3, 2017, www.cbs.com/shows/cbs-sunday-morning/video/DURL8wOwrT2WRSJw0X_fWo69VWASr1xD/harvey-a-disaster-of-biblical-proportions/.

[9]Greg Toppo, "'Cajun Navy' Heads to Texas to Aid Harvey Rescues," *USA Today*, August 27, 2017, www.usatoday.com/story/news/2017/08/27/cajun-navy-heads-texas-aid-rescues/606883001/.

[10]Federal Emergency Management Agency, "Historic Disaster Response to Hurricane Harvey in Texas," news release no. HQ-17-133, September 22, 2017, www.fema.gov/press-release/20210318/historic-disaster-response-hurricane-harvey-texas.

[11]White House Office of Faith-Based and Neighborhood Partnerships, *Partnerships for the Common Good,* Washington, DC: The White House, US Department of Health and Human Services, https://obamawhitehouse.archives.gov/sites/default/files/faithbasedtoolkit.pdf.

[12]National Hurricane Center, "Costliest US Tropical Cyclones Tables Updated," January 26, 2018, www.nhc.noaa.gov/news/UpdatedCostliest.pdf.

[13]"U.S.: Hurricane Harvey's Toll on Texas Energy," *Snapshots* (blog), Stratfor, August 28, 2017, https://worldview.stratfor.com/article/us-hurricane-harvey-s-toll-texas-energy.

[14]Steve Mufson, "Exxonmobil Refineries Are Damaged in Hurricane Harvey, Releasing Hazardous Pollutants," *The Washington Post*, August 29, 2017, www.washingtonpost.com/news/energy-environment/wp/2017/08/29/exxonmobil-refineries-damaged-in-hurricane-harvey-releasing-hazardous-pollutants.

[15]Clifford Krauss and Hiroko Tabuchi, "Harvey's Toll on Energy Industry Shows a Texas Vulnerability," *The New York Times*, August 29, 2017, www.nytimes.com/2017/08/29/business/energy-environment/harvey-energy-industry-texas.html; Frank Bajak and Lise Olsen, "Hurricane Harvey's Toxic Impact Deeper than Public Told," *AP News*, March 23, 2018, https://apnews.com/article/e0ceae76d5894734b0041210a902218d.

Reflection 5. Know the Family from Which You Were Formed

[1]Corrie Ten Boom, with Elizabeth Sherrill and John Sherrill, *The Hiding Place*, 35th anniversary ed. (Grand Rapids, MI: Chosen Books, 2006).

[2]Both Calvinist Cadet Corps and Calvinettes (now called GEMS) currently function as nondenominational organizations.

[3]Reformed Church in America, Heidelberg Catechism, approved by Synod 1975 of the Christian Reformed Church, www.crcna.org/welcome/beliefs/confessions/heidelberg-catechism. Verses cited are Exodus 34:7; Psalm 5:4-6; 7:11; Nahum 1:2; Romans 1:18; 5:12; Ephesians 5:6; Hebrews 9:27; Galatians 3:10; Deuteronomy 27:26.

[4]So as not to take anything out of context, here is the teaching of Lord's Day 3 in its entirety from the Heidelberg Catechism:

6. Q. Did God, then, create man so wicked and perverse?

A. No, on the contrary, God created man good[1] and in his image,[2] that is, in true righteousness and holiness,[3] so that he might rightly know God his Creator,[4] heartily love him, and live with him in eternal blessedness to praise and glorify him.[5]

[1]Gen 1:31.
[2]Gen 1:26-27.
[3]Eph 4:24.
[4]Col 3:10.
[5]Ps 8.

7. Q. From where, then, did man's depraved nature come?

A. From the fall and disobedience of our first parents, Adam and Eve, in Paradise,[1] for there our nature became so corrupt[2] that we are all conceived and born in sin.[3]

[1]Gen 3.
[2]Rom 5:12, 18-19.
[3]Ps 51:5.

8. Q. But are we so corrupt that we are totally unable to do any good and inclined to all evil?

A. Yes,[1] unless we are regenerated by the Spirit of God.[2]

[1]Gen 6:5; 8:21; Job 14:4; Is 53:6.
[2]Jn 3:3-5.

Reformed Church in America, Heidelberg Catechism

Reflection 6. Christ's Community Spans Faith Traditions

[1]Todd M. Johnson, David B. Barrett, and George Thomas Kurian, *World Christian Encyclopedia: A Comparative Survey of Churches and Religions in the Modern World*, 2nd ed. (New York: Oxford University Press, 2001) 1:16, Table 1-5.

[2]Sebastian Junger, "The Terror of Sierra Leone," *Vanity Fair*, December 8, 2006, www.vanityfair.com/news/2000/08/junger200008.

Reflection 7. The World Exists in the City

[1]Diana Whitney and David Cooperrider, *Appreciative Inquiry: A Positive Revolution in Change* (San Francisco: Berrett-Koehler Publishers, 2005).

[2]James Ludema and Bernard Mohr, *The Appreciative Inquiry Summit: A Practitioner's Guide for Leading Large-Group Change* (San Francisco: Berrett-Koehler Publishers, 2003).

Reflection 8. *Together We Can Transform the World*

[1]Kate Etue and Jenny Eaton, eds., *The aWAKE Project: Uniting Against the African AIDS Crisis* (Nashville: W. Publishing Group, 2002).

[2]World Health Organization, "Listings of WHO's Response to Covid-19," December 28, 2020, www.who.int/news/item/29-06-2020-covidtimeline.

[3]Jeanna Bryner, "1st Known Case of Coronavirus Traced Back to November in China," Live Science, March 14, 2020, www.livescience.com /first-case-coronavirus-found.html.

[4]J. Coffin et al., "What to Call the AIDS Virus?" *Nature* 321, no. 6065 (May 1986): 10, https://doi.org/10.1038/321010a0.

[5]Princess Kasune Zulu with Belinda Collins, *Warrior Princess: Fighting for Life with Courage and Hope*, (Downers Grove, IL: InterVarsity Press, 2010).

Reflection 10. *God Is Already at Work in the Church There*

[1]Pew Research Center, "The Future of World Religions: Population Growth Projections, 2010-2050," April 2, 2015, https://assets.pewresearch .org/wp-content/uploads/sites/11/2015/03/PF_15.04.02_ProjectionsFull Report.pdf, 43, 59-60.

[2]"What Is Evangelical Fellowship of Zimbabwe?" Who We Are, Evangelical Fellowship of Zimbabwe, September 21, 2017, www.efzimbabwe .org/who-we-are.

[3]Living Water International, *Flourish: Mobilizing Churches and Communities for Wash-Focused Transformation*, 2 vols. (Stafford, TX: Living Water International, 2018). The Flourish Facilitator's Guide and Program Guide are available for download in English, Spanish, and French at https://water.cc/flourish/.

[4]David C. Kirkpatrick, "C. René Padilla and the origins of integral mission in post-war Latin America," *The Journal of Ecclesiastical History* 67, no. 2 (2016): 351-71.

[5]United Nations Economic Commission for Latin America and the Caribbean (ECLAC), *Honduras: Assessment of the Damage Caused by Hurricane Mitch, 1998* (Mexico, DF: ELAC, 1999), https://web.archive.org /web/20140519074125/http://www.eclac.org/publicaciones/xml/6/15506 /L367-1-EN.pdf.

[6]National Climatic Data Center, "Mitch: The Deadliest Atlantic Hurricane since 1780," United States National Oceanic and Atmospheric Administration, US Department of Commerce, January 23, 2009, https://web .archive.org/web/20120717103126/http:/lwf.ncdc.noaa.gov/oa/reports /mitch/mitch.html.

[7]World Health Organization, "1998—Hurricane Mitch, Update," Emergencies Preparedness, Response (website section), updated November 10, 1998. www.who.int/csr/don/1998_11_10a/en/.

[8]Eric N. Newberg, *Christians in South Indian Villages, 1959–2009: Decline and Revival in Telangana,* (2016), 135-37; Paul Fernandes, "Tracing St Bartholomew's Footsteps to Betalbatim," *Times of India,* September 10, 2017, https://timesofindia.indiatimes.com/city/goa/tracing-st-bartholomews -footsteps-to-betalbatim/articleshow/60447144.cms.

[9]James Kurikilamkatt, *First Voyage of the Apostle Thomas to India: Ancient Christianity in Bharuch and Taxila* (Adelaide, South Australia: ATF Press, 2007), 140.

[10]Parts of this story appear in Mission Frontiers Issue 35:5 (Sept/Oct 2013) as *Pentecost in Rajasthan: Water and Living Water in India* by Paul Dařílek (Living Water's then Director of Communications) and are recounted here with permission from the author.

Reflection 11. God Is Moving in the Church Here

[1]Pew Research Center Forum on Religion and Public Life, "'Nones' on the Rise," Pew Research, October 9, 2012, www.pewforum.org/2012/10/09 /nones-on-the-rise/.

[2]Barna Group, "Signs of Decline and Hope Among Key Metrics of Faith," State of the Church 2020, March 4, 2020, www.barna.com/research /changing-state-of-the-church/.

Note: In the study a *practicing Christian* is defined as "someone who identifies as Christian, agrees strongly that faith is important in their lives, and has attended church within the past month."

[3]Sugar Creek Baptist Church, "Dalton Havard Memories," 2016, 1:20-1:38, https://vimeo.com/178007777.

[4]Rick McKinley, Chris Seay, and Greg Holder, *Advent Conspiracy: Making Christmas Meaningful (Again)* (Grant Rapids, MI, Zondervan, 2018), 21-22.

[5]Rick McKinley, Chris Seay, and Greg Holder, *Advent Conspiracy: Making Christmas Meaningful (Again)* (Grand Rapids, MI, Zondervan, 2018); Keith Levy, "The Christmas Conspiracy: Spending Less = Giving More," *Forbes,* December 20, 2011, www.forbes.com/sites/keithlevy/2011/12/20 /the-christmas-conspiracy-spending-less-giving-more/?sh=5e91f54a6613; Rev. Aaron Graham, "Christmas Gifts and the Advent Conspiracy," *The Washington Post,* December 22, 2011, https://www.washingtonpost.com

/local/christmas-gifts-and-the-advent-conspiracy/2011/12/22/gIQA
P3LaBP_story.html; Wired Staff, "Advent Conspiracy: A Different Approach to the Holidays," *WIRED*, November 18, 2009, www.wired
.com/2009/11/advent-conspiracy-a-different-approach-to-the-holidays/;
Katelyn Beaty, "'Conspiracy' Resists Holiday Greed, Urges Giving," *Christianity Today*, December 11, 2007, www.christianitytoday.com/news/2007
/december/conspiracy-resists-holiday-greed-urges-giving.html; Fox
News, "'Advent Conspiracy' Seeks to Bring Back Meaning of Christmas,"
updated January 7, 2015, published December 18, 2009, www.foxnews
.com/us/advent-conspiracy-seeks-to-bring-back-meaning-of-christmas.

[6]"The Advent Conspiracy Movement" (map), Advent Conspiracy, accessed December 16, 2020, https://adventconspiracy.org/about/.

[7]"Liquid Church," OUTREACH 100, https://outreach100.com/churches
/liquid-church. Liquid Church appears in the list of top 100 fastest-growing churches in 2016, 2018, 2019, and 2020.

[8]Tim Lucas and Warren Bird, *Liquid Church: 6 Powerful Currents to Saturate Your City for Christ* (Grand Rapids, MI: Zondervan, 2019), 141.

Reflection 12. *So That We May Be One*

[1]Steve Corbett and Brian Fikkert, *When Helping Hurts: How to Alleviate Poverty Without Hurting the Poor . . . and Yourself* (Chicago: Moody, 2014).

[2]Bryant L. Myers, *Walking with the Poor: Principles and Practices of Transformational Development* (New York: Orbis Books, 2011).

[3]"Making Disciples of Oral Learners" Lausanne Occasional Paper 54, Lausanne Issue Group for Making Disciples of Oral Learners, 2004 Forum for World Evangelization, Pattaya, Thailand, www.lausanne.org
/content/lop/making-disciples-oral-learners-lop-54.

[4]"Who Are Oral Communicators?" International Orality Network, https://orality.net/about/who-are-oral-communicators/.

[5]https://orality.net.

[6]Greg Holder, *The Genius of One: God's Answer for Our Fractured World* (Colorado Springs: NavPress, 2017).

[7]K. Marshall, "The Role of Faith in the Human Capital Project," speech, World Bank Global Faith Initiative Roundtable, 2019 Spring Meetings of the World Bank Group, Washington, DC, April 9-13, 2019.

FIGURE CREDITS

ABOUT LIVING WATER INTERNATIONAL

L IVING WATER INTERNATIONAL links arms with churches around the world to serve thirsty communities through access to safe water, sanitation, and hygiene—and an experience of Living Water, which alone satisfies the deepest thirst.

Over the past thirty years, this shared mission has blessed more than six million people in twenty-seven countries, through 21,000 WASH (water, sanitation, and hygiene) projects that lead to physical and spiritual flourishing.

Church leaders across Africa, South Asia, Latin America, and the Caribbean partner with Living Water's global staff, one another, and other local stakeholders to activate the Church's kingdom vision and practical skills as they work together to transform their communities through WASH and the good news. Together, Living Water International and the local church help improve community health, education, and livelihoods while demonstrating and proclaiming God's love.

In North America, Living Water reaches out to church leaders to partner with Living Water's US staff and one another to mobilize their communities for crosscultural learning, engagement, discipleship, investment, and service through the global body of Christ.

Like this book, Living Water International invites the church to reflect Christ's unity across our rich diversity to serve together to end the water crisis while sharing the gospel of redemption and reconciliation.

To learn more visit http://water.cc.

ABOUT THE AUTHOR

Michael J. Mantel is president and CEO of Living Water International, a faith-based global humanitarian organization. Prior to 2008, he spent seventeen years working for World Vision and nine years in business. He holds a PhD in Organization Development from Benedictine University and lives in Houston with his wife, Natalie, with whom he raised four daughters.